Drive and Stroll

Essex

———•———

Len Banister

COUNTRYSIDE BOOKS
NEWBURY BERKSHIRE

First published 2004
© Len Banister 2004
Revised and updated 2010

COUNTRYSIDE BOOKS
3 Catherine Road
Newbury, Berkshire

To view our complete range of books,
please visit us at
www.countrysidebooks.co.uk

ISBN 978 1 85306 839 3

*Dedicated to the
memory of
Fred Matthews*

Photographs by the author
Cover photograph of Tollesbury marina
supplied by Robert Hallmann
Designed by Peter Davies, Nautilus Design

Produced through MRM Associates Ltd., Reading
Typeset by CJWT Solutions, St Helens
Printed by Information Press, Oxford

Contents ✑

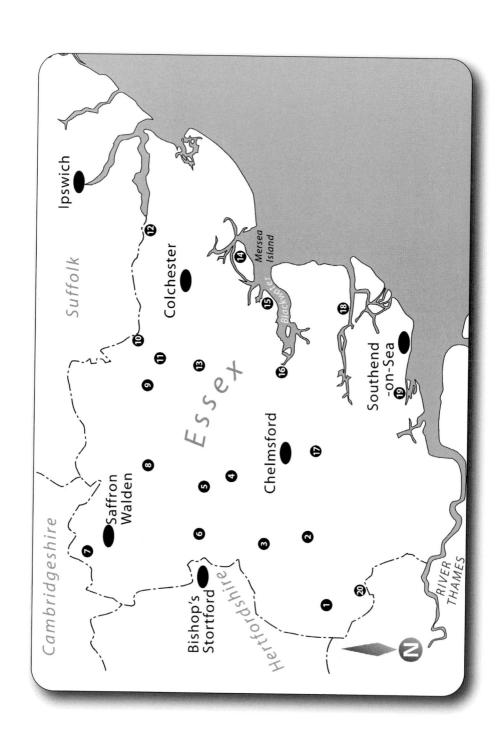

Contents ✍

PUBLISHER'S NOTE

We hope that you obtain considerable enjoyment from this book; great care has been taken in its preparation. Although at the time of publication all routes followed public rights of way or permitted paths, diversion orders can be made and permissions withdrawn.

We cannot, of course, be held responsible for such diversion orders and any inaccuracies in the text which result from these or any other changes to the routes nor any damage which might result from walkers trespassing on private property. We are anxious though that all details covering the walks are kept up to date and would therefore welcome information from readers which would be relevant to future editions.

The simple sketch maps that accompany the walks in this book are based on notes made by the author whilst checking out the routes on the ground. They are designed to show you how to reach the start, to point out the main features of the overall circuit and they contain a progression of numbers that relate to the paragraphs of the text.

However, for the benefit of a proper map, we do recommend that you purchase the relevant Ordnance Survey sheet covering your walk. The Ordnance Survey maps are widely available, especially through booksellers and local newsagents.

Introduction ✒

Essex may not have great mountains or extensive moors but it does have forests, lakes and an extraordinary coastline. Interspersed with all these delights are some magnificent grand houses, delightful villages and memorable pubs.

I lived on the edge of Essex for many years before I started walking there. I had visited most areas of Britain to walk during my holidays but never thought of pursuing my hobby locally until I came across a book by the late Norman Skinner in the Countryside Book series. This and subsequent books by Norman and others by Fred Matthews, another great pioneer of walking in Essex, led me on a fascinating journey of discovery.

Here, then, is my own selection of walks and each offers a glimpse of the variety to be found in Essex. The vast network of paths that criss-cross the county can be easily accessed from the many parking areas dotted about the countryside and for every route I have suggested a suitable car park (sometimes more than one) from which you can set off on your stroll.

The walks in this book are between 2½ and 6 miles, and, at the beginning of each walk, there is an idea of the time that each should take but do remember that the emphasis here is on 'stroll' with its advantages of having plenty of time to pause and admire the scenery or explore the places passed en route.

The route descriptions are very detailed and are accompanied by sketch maps, with numbering to match the numbered points in the text. It would be possible, therefore, for you to complete each walk without an Ordnance Survey map but you might like to take the relevant OS sheet with you and plan your own variations on these themes.

All the paths and tracks used are public rights of way, so if you keep to the routes you will have no trouble. Farmers are generally very good at leaving paths clear across fields but I have often included directions to enable you to find your way even if the path is not obvious on the ground. Please help farmers by leaving gates as you find them and making sure that you take your litter home.

I hope that the trips inspired by this book will bring some new experiences and that you will take every opportunity, as I do, of strolling in the Essex countryside.

Len Banister

1 | High Beach, Epping Forest

The magnificent Grimston's Oak at the end of point 2

The Walk 3¾ miles ⏱ 2 hours
Map OS Explorer 174 Epping Forest & Lee Valley GR 408967

How to get there

Leave the M25 at junction 26 and take the road towards Loughton. Turn off on the A104 to the Robin Hood roundabout. Go right here signposted to High Beach and take the first left (there is a tea hut and car park on the corner); our parking area is about ⅓ mile down the hill on the right. **Alternatively** you could park directly off the A104 at the end of point 7 (so your walk would start at point 8) – however, this may be difficult to locate if there is much pressure from traffic.

Drive and Stroll

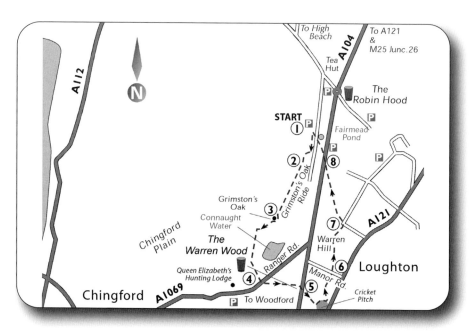

Introduction

Epping Forest is one of those big Victorian philanthropic ideas for which the whole of East London will be eternally grateful. After many long and involved legal battles, the Corporation of London was appointed Conservator of the 2,400 hectares in 1878. Most of the Forest is now designated a Site of Special Scientific Interest and it supports a wide variety of habitats: woodland, lakes, grass and heathland.

The real delight of the area is in its exploration by the myriad of paths, which probably originated as deer runs. On this occasion, however, as an introduction, we will stick mainly to the obvious paths, known as 'rides', which have been prepared for horse riders.

Refreshments

You pass the Warren Wood pub (020 8503 3737) at the end of point 4 but no visit to this part of the Forest is complete without visiting one of the 'tea huts'. You will have passed one when you approached the parking place – this is usually the haunt of bikers, a friendly bunch, many in their sixties. If you are not interested in examining the wonderful gleaming machines on display, go left then right to High Beach where there is another hut with views over to Waltham Abbey.

THE WALK

(1)

Leave the car park and turn right down the narrow road. Soon you will have continuous woodland on your right. When you come to barrier gates on each side of the road, turn right on a good, surfaced ride.

(2)

At a major junction of paths fork left. After about ⅓ mile this straight path splits up to form a circular track. In the centre is **Grimston's Oak**.

This magnificent tree is known to be at least 400 years old. It has had several names, in the 1880s a well-known cricketer called Grimston was instrumental in having the area around the tree cleared.

(3)

Go left around the oak and keep forward. At the next major junction turn left and continue along a wide surfaced drive. At the end you cross over the **Cuckoo Brook** to confront another major crossroads – ahead is **Chingford Plain** but you go left on a surfaced path, which takes you to **Ranger's Road**.

(4)

Cross with care to go past a barrier and then immediately turn left on a narrow path that takes you, by an earth bridge, over the **Ching**. Look ahead and you will see a line of white posts going up the hill – follow these and, at the top, pick up your direction from a waymarker bearing the green symbol of the **London Loop**, swinging right towards houses (stop here and turn round to get a good view of **Chingford Plain** and **Chingford Green**). A second waymarker directs you across the road but, if climbing the hill has made you thirsty, you may wish to visit the **Warren Wood** pub, which is to your right.

The London Loop is a near-circular path around Greater London.

(5)

Cross the A104 (**Epping New Road**) with care to a waymarker on the other side. Go right at a fork and into trees to emerge on a cricket pitch. Turn left to pass a creosoted hut and skirt the pitch. By a low bench you will see a path just inside the trees on your left – join this and then go left on a surfaced track. This track, which is joined by another from the left, descends to **Manor Road**.

(6)

Cross to the path opposite and, ignoring all side paths, go down into a dip and climb up the other side. At the top you will be confronted with **Ovist's Oak**.

This tree was named after a superintendent of the Forest. It's a good example of a mature pollarded oak. Pollarding involves the periodic lopping off of branches 6 to 9 feet above the ground to harvest the wood for poles and fuel. The advantage of pollarding over coppicing, which involves cutting at almost ground level, is that the new shoots are out of the reach of browsing animals.

A thoughtfully placed mounting block

Go past the oak on the main track, which soon descends to a prominent red post box. When you arrive here you will see that you have reached a corner forming the junction of **Warren Hill** and **Nursery Road**.

 (7)

Go half left across the corner to re-enter Forest land. Keep to the main ride, ignoring a minor fork off to the right, until you reach a small parking area. Go left to cross the main road with care.

The fencing here is relatively recent and was installed when cattle were reintroduced to the Forest. Prior to concerns about BSE, the grazing of cattle had largely maintained the balance between wood and grassland, and it was not uncommon to find the odd cow holding up a long line of traffic or to see a herd invading streets of nearby Chingford. The new herd, of English Longhorns, is strictly controlled with temporary fencing.

 (8)

Go through a swing gate and turn right before a thoughtfully placed mounting block, then aim for a white post in the distance to your left, following the path on the ground. On reaching the post swing right, passing to the left of **Fairmead Pond**, and continue to the road and car park.

2 Chipping Ongar

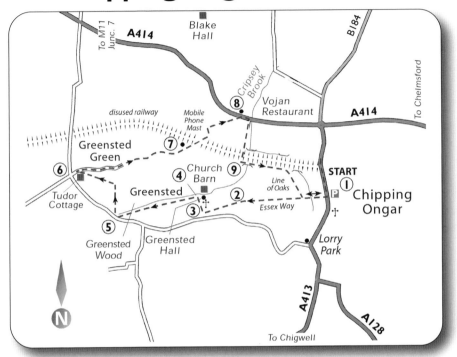

The Walk 4¼ miles ⏲ 3 hours (allowing time to visit the church)
Map OS Explorer 183 Chelmsford & The Rodings GR 553032

How to get there

Chipping Ongar can be reached by the A414 from junction 7 of the M11 or via the A113 from Chigwell. The car parks are to the north of the town on opposite sides of the road. The long-stay car park by the library is cheaper (free on Saturday and Sunday) if you are parking for more than two hours. **Alternatively** park in the lorry park for free, opposite the Two Brewers pub, about ¼ mile south-west of the start. You would then have the advantage of walking through the town before the walk proper.

Drive and Stroll

Introduction

Chipping Ongar is like a bustling market town without a market. It offers lots of pleasant shops, a good range of well-preserved buildings, a castle mound and an association with Dr David Livingstone, the Victorian hero.

This walk takes you out of Ongar to an ancient church and then to a home of ex-criminals. Linking these delights are some exceptional covered lanes, which occasionally reveal good views across the surrounding countryside. You may even see a kingfisher.

Refreshments

There are plenty of pubs and cafés in Ongar. Alongside your starting point, and part of Budworth Hall, is the Clock Tower café and restaurant. Here on one hand you can sit down to afternoon tea or order filled baguettes or straightforward fish and chips – on the other you can go for the more sophisticated fare like confit duck leg with chilli and bitter orange sauce served with sautéed potatoes or filo parcel filled with feta cheese and spinach on a bed of marinated red peppers (telephone: 01277 362431).

THE WALK

Leave the car park and walk down **Banson's Lane**, with Sainsbury's on your left, to cross a bridge over the **Cripsey Brook**. Go forward past some small trees on your left to join the edge of the large field. As the hedge bends away, carry straight on along a clear track.

You are now on part of the Essex Way. This is a long-distance footpath that travels from Epping in the south-west to the port of Harwich in the north-east. Following ancient green lanes and footpaths, it is 81 miles long.

The path just kisses the hedge then continues forward towards a gap in the line of trees ahead.

Go over duckboards through the gap, then across a drive through a kissing gate into a field. Walk up the fenced right-hand edge and continue to the right of the next field.

Now the ornamental pond and gardens of Greensted Hall are in full view on the right. In a few moments you will see the Hall itself ahead.

Towards the end of the field veer left through a sprung wooden gate

Chipping Ongar

past the delightful **Church Lodge** to reach a drive.

↰ ③

Turn right then right again to enter the churchyard.

St Andrew's church, Greensted, is thought by many to be the oldest wooden church in the world. As you can see, its walls are made of vertical oak tree trunks split in half and erected so that the curved surface is on the outside. It was built on the site of an earlier Saxon church after the Norman Conquest in the late 11th century. As you enter the churchyard, on your left, you will see the remains of a wooden cross marking the grave of a local drover who bled to death as a result of using his scythe on the roadside after a bout of drinking.

This marks the drover's grave

Continue your walk by leaving the churchyard and turning right. Swing left to pass converted barns and join a concrete trackway which you follow to cross a bridge on the left.

④

Walk along the right-hand edge of this and the next field. The third field is reached by a bridge and the hedge is replaced by **Greensted Wood**. At the final corner, cross a plank bridge and go through a barrier to a road.

⑤

Turn right and cross the entrance to **Greensted Wood Farm** and, after about 15 yards, find a signed path on your right. This takes you across a bridge, another barrier and up the left side of a plantation of young trees. At the end, go through the hedge and take the left of the two paths. This pleasant meandering, shady path passes through scrub and woodland to emerge, over gravel, in the tiny hamlet of **Greensted Green**. Walk to the lane.

The last house on the left is Tudor Cottage. As a small plaque testifies, some of the Tolpuddle Martyrs lived here. They were six Dorset farmworkers who had the temerity to object to their low wages and formed one of the first trade unions. They were taken to court in 1834, convicted and condemned to transportation to Australia for seven years where they worked on a chain gang. There was a massive public outcry at the sentences, which, as a result, were commuted

in 1837. The Dorset farmers would not allow the rebel farmworkers back but they were granted tenancies in Greensted and High Laver. The tenancies were not renewed because of local opposition and they eventually emigrated to Ontario, Canada.

⑥

Turn right in the lane and, at its end, continue forward to join a beautiful covered path with views over countryside to the left and ponds on the right. Ignore all side turnings to arrive at cottages after about ½ mile.

⑦

Continue along what is now a track towards a mobile phone mast to cross a railway bridge.

Most disused railways have long since lost their rails – not so the line to Chipping Ongar from Epping. A team of volunteers has been working hard to upgrade the infrastructure so that the occasional steam train can transport visitors.

Keep to the track, and when it swings left you will see opposite, up on the valley side, the pristine white building of **Blake Hall**.

Blake Hall was built for the Capel Cure family in 1786. The gardens, which cover 25 acres, are open from spring until autumn. They feature an ice house, an ancient

Tudor cottage, once home to the Tolpuddle Martyrs

barn, a large tropical house,
herbaceous borders, wild areas and
a duck pond. Visitors are welcome
to picnic within the peaceful
surroundings (telephone: 01277
366687).

Eventually you reach the main
road (A414) by an isolated Indian
restaurant called **Vojan**.

Turn right and immediately before
the bridge turn right again to join
the left-hand edge of a field.

*You are now walking along the
edge of the Cripsey Brook. Lots of
people tell me that you can see
kingfishers here. I have walked this
section many times, enjoying the
variety of flowers. I have seen an
owl, dragonflies and eaten sloes
and blackberries – but I have never
seen a kingfisher!*

About 20 yards before the end of
the brook-side path, where you see
a hedge ahead, turn right to go
under a railway bridge

Turn sharp left to cross a bridge to
walk up the edge of the field with
the railway on your left. Just before
a solitary tree go right to follow a
line of oaks. **Ongar church spire** is
now on the skyline. At a cross-track
turn left and retrace your outward
journey to the car park.

3 | Matching Green

The church and church house at Matching

The Walk 4 miles ⏰ 2½ hours
Map OS Explorer 183 Chelmsford & The Rodings GR 535110

How to get there

Matching Green can be approached from junction 7 of the M11 or from the A1060. There are a myriad of narrow roads in this area but the signposts are good. Once you get to Matching Green, circle the green until you spot the Chequers pub. Park on the edge of the green near the pub.

Drive and Stroll

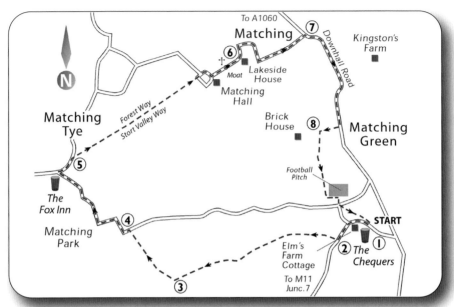

Introduction

On this walk you have a chance to see some peaceful villages surprisingly near to the M11. The Matchings are two villages and a hamlet that derive their names from the Saxons, for whom *ing* meant meadow and *Moecca* was the tribe – so on this walk we are visiting the meadows of the Moecca. It is thought that the Moecca arrived to settle near the site of the present Matching church after the Romans had left in the 5th century.

Matching Green, where we start, is dominated by its vast grassed central area. Closer inspection reveals two ponds and some scrub well away from the road and it is a fairly common sight to see a heron moving from one pond to another. The whole green is surrounded with interesting houses ranging in styles of the last five centuries. Right at the start of the walk, next to the pub, you will pass the former home of the famous British painter Augustus John.

Refreshments

The Chequers in Matching Green – a remodelled pub where the emphasis is on food – is hard to beat. It is best to book, especially at weekends – closed on Mondays (telephone: 01279 731276). If you want a more traditional, walker-friendly but no less interesting pub, the **Fox Inn** with its collection of dye-cast cars and vans, which you will pass at Matching Tye, should fit the bill (telephone: 01279 731335).

THE WALK

NB: About a third of this walk is along country lanes. Although there is little traffic it is important that walkers adopt safe practice. Normally, walk on the right-hand side of the road so that you are facing the oncoming traffic – cross over to the left-hand side when you approach a right-hand bend.

①

Walk along the road with the **Chequers** pub on your left.

A blue plaque on the next house indicates the ex-residence of Augustus John.

At the first junction, turn left down past **Elm's Farm Cottage** and continue for about 200 yards.

 ②

Look for a stile by a metal gate on the right and go across a field to another stile, where you enter a long narrow field and aim for the far right-hand corner. Now bend down and climb through a wide fence, then walk over a bridge to go along the right field edge. At the field corner, continue to the left-hand edge of a strip of woodland and then carry straight on with the wood on your right to, once again, go straight on across an open field to a bridge.

 ③

Go forward to a corner and turn right at a waymarker post, then keep to the field edge and pass another waymarker. Now keep to the right-hand edge of the field and come to a road.

 ④

Turn left and follow the road for about ½ mile to enter **Matching Tye**.

On your way you pass Matching Park, a glorious wood to which, unfortunately, there is no public access. In Matching Tye there are more attractive houses, a pub and a small green.

When you reach the village sign with the **Fox Inn** on your left take the right fork and follow the road as it curves left. About 30 yards after the last house on the right, look for a finger-post on the right, directing you up the straight right edge of a massive field.

 ⑤

Keep to this path for over ½ mile to reach a lane and turn right. Follow the lane round as it makes its way through **Matching** with the **church of St Mary the Virgin** on the left and **Matching Hall** on the right.

The most memorable part of this walk will undoubtedly be your first sight of the hamlet of Matching. The church, the moated manor house and associated buildings along with the large oak tree form a truly idyllic scene – surely one of the most beautiful in Essex. If the weather is fine, this is an excellent spot to stop for a period of contemplation or just to explore. The present church dates from the 13th century, having been built on the site of a Saxon timber church. The building to the left is a Marriage Feast Room dating from 1480. The oak tree, which is now about 4 yards in circumference, was planted to mark Queen Victoria's Jubilee in 1887.

The house of Augustus John

 (6)

The lane goes downhill and turns sharply right to pass between two lakes. It then goes right again to climb above the lake on your right, giving you a good view of the lakeside house with its veranda. Keep with the lane until you reach a T-junction.

 (7)

Turn right on this road, passing the entrance to **Kingston's Farm**, and continue for about ½ mile to turn right down the 'Private Road' to **Brick House**.

 (8)

At the first hedge, turn left to walk along with the hedge on your right. Eventually you will reach a football pitch – go past this, turning left and soon right to walk up a fenced path. You now emerge on the side of **Matching Green** and if you look diagonally left you will see the **Chequers**. You can walk across the green or, alternatively, go round it in a clockwise direction to examine the splendid houses.

4 | Pleshey

Cottages in Pleshey

The Walk 3 miles 🕐 1½ hours
Map OS Explorer 183 Chelmsford & The Rodings GR 663143

How to get there

Pleshey is signposted from the A1060, which runs from Bishop's Stortford to Chelmsford, and from the A130 at Ford End between Chelmsford and Great Dunmow. Just west of the church at the southern end of Pleshey is the village hall, with a large car park alongside.

Drive and Stroll

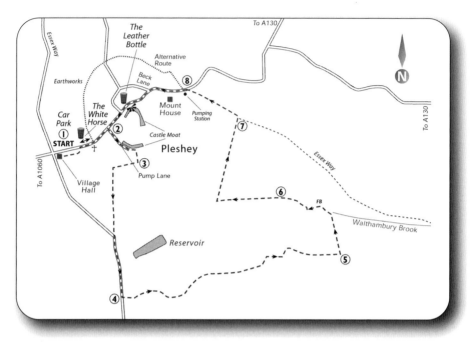

Introduction

A glance at the map will show that the whole of **Pleshey** is dominated by the ramparts of what is one of Essex's best examples of an earth-built Norman motte and bailey castle. This walk provides views of the castle remains, now in private hands, and some glimpses of the moat. It goes on to take us above the village through some lovely hedged lanes before returning to pass through the beautiful village itself, with a chance to admire the delightful houses. Alternatively, you can finish the stroll by tracing the outer limits of the castle on a signed footpath

This is an easy route – it is short, simple and the quality of the paths used is good – and you will be left in no doubt as to why Pleshey is derived from *plaisy*, a pleasant village.

Refreshments

There are two pubs in Pleshey. The White Horse (telephone: 01245 237281) is near the church and is a cheerful place in a 15th century building where superior meals are served. If you fancy a traditional pub, the Leather Bottle (telephone: 01245 237291) is a gem – especially the public bar with its plain walls and furniture.

THE WALK

①

Walk out of the car park and turn right, passing **Pleshey church** on the right and the **White Horse** on your left to go right at **Pump Lane**.

②

Follow the lane round to the left, skirting the castle moat. After a few yards you come to a bridge across the moat to a gate. Unless you have arranged a private visit the view from the gate is the only significant one you can gain of the central castle remains.

The castle was built in the mid 12th century by Geoffrey de Mandeville. The northern bailey is now marked by the curving line of Back Lane. In the late 12th century there was a second phase of building, probably as a result of the granting of permission to refortify the castle in 1167. The enclosure is semi-circular in plan, surrounding an area of about 14 hectares, the castle itself forming the southern limit. (For an appointment to view, telephone: 01245 360239.)

All too soon the circuit of the castle ends and you have to turn right at a brick-built barn.

③

At a T-junction, turn right on a concrete track and keep with it as it swings left at the end of the field to continue with a hedge on the right. Before reaching the bottom of the field the track is joined by another coming in from the right. There are now hedges on both sides. Go past a footpath sign pointing to a reservoir on the left and continue to climb the gentle slope on the concrete path until you come to a second finger-post.

④

Turn left onto the bridleway.

From this path you will get good views of the church near your starting point. Occasionally you may just be able to get glimpses of the castle mounds, although these are not nearly as obvious as when it was built. Apart from the effects of erosion the walls would have been topped by tall palisades.

You will continue on this track for ¾ mile, ignoring all side turns. Soon the track becomes hedged.

These lanes are particularly attractive in early autumn when the leaves are changing colour. The low sunlight shining through the incomplete canopy produces a dappled effect, and at the same time you have partial protection from the cold winds associated with this time of the year.

⑤

Turn left at some white-topped waymarker posts to leave one track and join another, with the hedge on your left. Near the bottom of the field go left over a footbridge and right along the field edge. At a gap before some willows, cross the ditch and resume your direction in the next field, now with the ditch on your left.

Tt the end of the field cross a plank bridge with one handrail and continue forward to the end of this field. Here turn right to walk up the side of the field towards telephone wires, with the hedge on your left.

Here, and earlier, you will have noticed small feeding hoppers. These contain grain for the birds, mainly partridge in this location, that are being reared for the shoots by which farmers can supplement their income. Low fences of chicken wire around areas of scrub and woodland are also used to limit the movement of the birds and their predators. These gamebirds are not the most intelligent of beasts and will often wait until you are almost on top of them before flying off in a panic – the shock this causes often doubles my heartbeat.

Pass under the wires and continue down to the **Walthambury Brook**.

Turn left (you are now on the **Essex Way**) to eventually pass to the right of a pumping station and emerge on a road.

If you wish to follow the old boundaries of the castle (see map) you should cross to the signed footpath and continue alongside the outer wall. You will return to the road near the **White Horse** where you should turn right to reach the village hall.

The main route, however, takes you through the village to look at the houses.

Turn left on the road and walk up through the village. Almost immediately you pass the recently renovated **Mount House** with its collection of garden statuary. The other houses in the village are rather more modest but no less attractive. Soon after passing **Back Lane** you come to lines of pretty cottages on either side of the street. In the summer they are festooned with hanging baskets. Just beyond them is the **Leather Bottle** pub and, on the left, **Pleshey Mount** viewpoint. The latter is a pleasant area with seating on a lawn by a section of the castle moat. An information board gives a brief history of the castle and the village.

Pass **Pump Lane** to rejoin your outward route back to the village hall.

You may notice, at the end of the lane, the affectionately restored village pump.

5 | Little Dunmow

A magnificent road bridge over the abandoned railway

The Walk 2½ miles ⏲ 2 hours (allowing time to visit the priory)
Map OS Explorer 195 Braintree & Saffron Walden GR 657214

How to get there

Little Dunmow is east of Great Dunmow and is reached by a turning off the A120 onto the B1256 toward Great Dunmow, going right at a roundabout, then taking a signposted right turn. There is no designated parking in the village. The walk starts along Grange Lane, which is to the south of the Flitch of Bacon pub; the road widens just beyond this so you can park without causing an obstruction.

Drive and Stroll

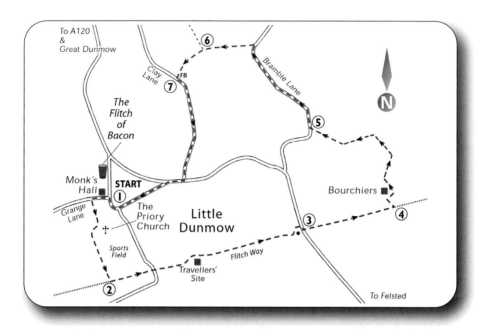

Introduction

During the first part of this short walk you amble along one of the best sections of the Flitch Way, a disused railway track (see Walk 6). Later you climb gently over open land to savour views before returning on another perfect covered way.

But this is Flitch Country and a visit wouldn't be complete without finding out something about this intriguing custom, which started in **Little Dunmow** and was famous in the middle of the 14th century, being alluded to by Chaucer in his *Wife of Bath*. The modern Flitch Ceremony is held every four years – these days in Great Dunmow – when a flitch or gammon of bacon is presented to a couple who have remained constant for a year and a day. The ceremony involves the couple reciting a poem, which begins:

> We do swear by custom of confession
> That we ne'er made nuptial transgression ...

The participants are then paraded in a splendidly carved chair, the original of which can still be seen in Little Dunmow church.
Little Dunmow, on edge of the River Chelmer valley, is a small scattered village with just a pub, the Priory and Vineyard, but has a great claim to fame: it is responsible for the phrase 'save my bacon' entering into the English language.

Refreshments

The Flitch of Bacon in Little Dunmow is the obvious choice on this occasion. This pleasant 17th century pub offers a good range of real ales and simple meals, which are cooked on the premises. The full text of the Flitch Poem is displayed here, and you can also look at literature associated with the Priory Church and borrow the keys if you wish (telephone: 01371 820323).

THE WALK

NB: You can shorten the walk slightly by turning left instead of right at point 5 (see map) but you will miss the best views.

Walk along Grange Lane passing **Monk's Hall** on your right and turn left onto a gravel path that eventually runs alongside the **Priory Church**, the keys to which are held at the **Flitch of Bacon**.

The church, which originated in the 12th century, was largely destroyed in 1536. The present building contains a font that is mainly 14th century, a 13th century coffin lid and a couple of 15th century tombs. The main item of interest, however, is the Flitch Chair. This has got carved decoration on one side but not on the other, so was probably the end of a row of 13th century stalls made into a single chair in the 15th century. It was originally used in the Flitch Ceremony but has now been replaced by a replica, to be seen in St Mary's church, Great Dunmow. In 1930 the chair was included in an exhibition of 'English Medieval Art' at the Victoria and Albert Museum.

Continue on the gravel path and turn left just before the gates to a house. Walk alongside railings to go forward on a fenced path.

You now enter a sports field. Go straight on, keeping close to the hedge on your right. Continue ahead through an outcrop of trees to reach the **Flitch Way** at a T-junction.

Turn left. In late summer, besides blackberries, you can gather apples and damsons along this section. After a couple of minutes you will pass under a magnificent road bridge. A little later you will encounter a permanent travellers' site ahead. Here you fork left, down some steps and across a wooden bridge, to walk alongside the caravans. You next arrive at a tarmac area.

This was once the forecourt of the station shared by Little Dunmow and Felsted. The station, which is on the right, is now a private residence.

Cross slightly to the left to rejoin the path, which almost immediately goes down steps into a road.

Turn right, go between the remains of a railway bridge and cross over to walk up a slope and reach the track bed once again. In rather less than ¼ mile you will come to a small clearing with a cross-track. Here, over on your right, you can see **Felsted church** and its school – you will have better views of these later in the walk.

Turn left up towards a black wooden building with **Bourchiers farm** on your left. After 30 yards, cross a stile on the right to another in the fence opposite. Turn left and, at the corner of the fence, go diagonally right across the field to a bridge. Now go slightly diagonally left across the next field. At the field edge, go left to walk with the hedge to your right. Reach a concrete track and go right. Continue to a lane.

If you wanted to shorten the walk you could turn left here and follow the lane until you reached a road, where you would turn right to return to the start.

For the main route, however, you turn right and follow this lane for about ¼ mile. For the next ten

Monk's Hall at the start of the walk

minutes or so the walk is at its highest. Make sure that you stop now and then to take in the views.

You are now near the A120, which has recently been drastically modified. The original road was built on the site of Stane Street, a Roman road.

You will go under power lines and 100 yards after passing a plank bridge on your right you take a broad track on the left with a hedge on your right.

When this track swings right towards the A120, keep forward on a wide, grassy cross-field path. At the end of this go over a bridge with a metal rail.

Turn left on the delightful **Clay Lane**. All too soon you reach a road where you turn right, shortly forking left at a sign to **Little Dunmow**. Keep to this road to find where you have parked your car.

6 Hatfield Forest

Park opposite this Tudor barn in Takeley

The Walk 5 miles ⏱3 hours
Maps The walk is on the borders of two maps: OS Explorer 195 Braintree & Saffron Walden and 183 Chelmsford & The Rodings GR 547212

How to get there

Leave the M11 at junction 8A and follow the B1256 towards Takeley. The starting point is about 2 miles along the road, just before the second turning on the right (signposted to Bush End and Hatfield Forest). Approaching from Great Dunmow, cross the light controlled main junction at Takeley and, after nearly a mile, stop just past the Green Man. Park in a layby opposite an attractive Tudor barn with black beams. **Alternatively** you could park in Hatfield Forest itself. Go through the first car park and you will eventually arrive at a second – this is mentioned at the end of point 4 below.

Drive and Stroll

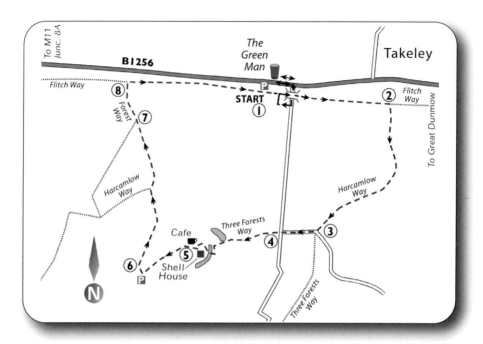

Introduction

Hatfield is the third, but possibly the least known, of the Essex Royal Forests. Like Epping and Hainault, it is a survival of a medieval hunting forest and still supports a population of fallow deer. Each forest has its own special characteristic – Hatfield's is the juxtaposition of trees and plains to make up the chases and rides. It survives because, in 1923, a dying landowner and naturalist, Edward Buxton, wrote his last cheque to purchase it. In the following year his sons gave the Forest to the National Trust.

On this walk you will see an attractive lake, which supports good coarse fishing and a wide variety of waterfowl, and the Shell House, a charming mid 18th century picnic room, decorated (as its name suggests) with shells and flints. However, the most enjoyable part should be strolling up the long, wide rides. Near our parking place you can examine a wide array of attractive Tudor to Georgian architecture. We start and finish the walk along the Flitch Way, part of a 15 mile long dismantled railway track that runs from Bishop's Stortford to Braintree (for an explanation of 'Flitch' see Walk 5).

Refreshments

The walk starts and finishes at the Green Man, a welcoming pub with a good range of basic bar food and an excellent selection of real ales (telephone: 01279 870367). The National Trust café near the lake sells a wide range of snacks, including baked potatoes, wood-cutter's sandwiches and 'pig in the poke' (Broad Oak sausage bapped and garnished).

THE WALK

Walk along the road with the **Green Man** on your left and then turn right up a lane signposted to **Bush End** and **Hatfield Forest**. Go under a bridge and immediately turn right up a path (not across a stile) and follow it up a steep bank. At the top, turn right to go over the bridge you have just passed under (you are now on the **Flitch Way**). After about ½ mile, at a yellow waymarked cross-track, go right.

Take this to walk up the left-hand edge of a field (this is part of the **Harcamlow Way**). At the field margin go straight on, still with the hedge on the left as the path swings gently round to the right (later, with glimpses of a lake on the left). At the end of the field, ignore the track to the left and keep with the field edge on a broad green path for 20 yards to turn left through a small gap indicated by a white-topped waymarker. Go over a concrete bridge. At a cross-track go left, then right to head for a stile. In the next field go diagonally left to another stile by a metal gate to emerge in a lane.

The Harcamlow Way is a 63 mile walking route that links Cambridge to Harlow.

Turn right (notice the pargeted swans on the house on the left) and continue over a bridge and up a gentle hill to reach and cross a road to a stile.

Pargeting is the raised plasterwork that decorates many old houses in the south. It seems to be particularly popular in Essex, to the extent that some new houses are now enhanced with the technique.

Go forward on a track, then over a stile by a wooden gate into woodland and follow the sign left to the lake. Keep forward on the main track and turn left at the lake edge. Swing around right with the path to cross in front of the **Shell House** and then left past the café and lavatories to reach a car park.

Hatfield was designated as a Royal Hunting Forest by Henry I. The lake was created in 1746 and the Shell House built a little later. Alongside the lakeside picnic area is a sheltered place with benches and tables where you can eat on

wet or windy days.
A mural in the
shelter describes
and illustrates the
history of the
region.

A pleasant place for a picnic

 ⑤
Leave the car
park to go
diagonally right to
a decapitated tree
by a bank (passing
a solitary oak on
your right). Once
you reach this, go
slightly left towards
a tall evergreen,
then cross two
plank bridges and walk forward up
the clearing until you reach a cross-track. Here, look ahead and walk
towards a wide opening which is
100 yards to the right of a wooden
coral to follow a waymarker with a
green disc to the right of some
scrub – walk to this. Now follow
the arrow to the right fork in
the paths.

*You are now on another long-distance walk – the Three Forests
Way – which, at 25 miles, links all
three Royal Forests.*

 ⑥
Keep forward to join a wide (8 yard)
track, with drainage ditches on each
side, which you will follow for about
a mile (you are likely to see deer in
the woodland on this part of the
walk). Ignore cross-tracks and side
turns until the broad track seems to
end in a track T-junction.

 ⑦
Turn left with a green-disked
waymarker and keep forward to
emerge in a clearing. Go half
clockwise around a clump of trees
ahead and make for the right-hand
corner of the clearing and what is
an information board beyond the
gap in the scrub. Leave by a gate.

 ⑧
Turn right (you are now back on
the **Flitch Way**) and keep to this
path for about a mile. Just before
the metal bridge, turn off right
down a steep slope to a lane. Turn
left to return to the main road and
your parking place.

7 Newport

Newport High Street

The Walk 6 miles ⏱ 3 hours
Map OS Explorer 195 Braintree & Saffron Walden GR 522345

How to get there

Newport is on the B1383, which runs between Great Chesterford and Bishop's Stortford and can be accessed by junctions 8 or 9 of the M11. Turn off eastwards down Bridge End, which is a narrow road to the north of the town. Fork right under the railway arch into Water Lane. Ahead to the right you will see a clear parking area with room for about five cars. **Alternatively** there is generally room at the station pay and display car park, where the rate is cheaper after 9.30 am. Parking here would mean that you start the walk at point 11.

Drive and Stroll

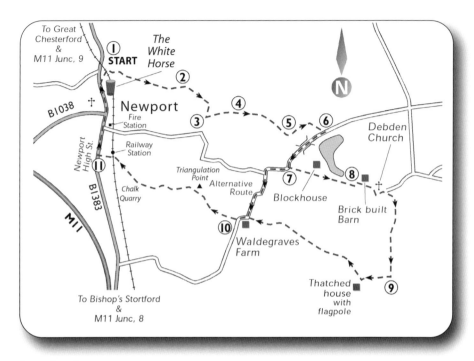

Introduction

This interesting walk has four distinct phases. We start out along the valley of Debden Water with a striking contrast between the flood plain of the river and the cultivated and wooded valley sides. Later we enter the manicured landscape of Debden Park with its extensive grassland and carefully positioned trees and lake. For our return we use an exposed ridge with expansive fields on both sides and views across into Hertfordshire. Finally we walk along the entire length of **Newport** High Street. This gives us the chance to admire the marvellous collection of buildings, which rivals, on a smaller scale, the better known examples of Long Melford and Lavenham in Suffolk.

Refreshments

Towards the end of the walk you will pass the White Horse public house (telephone: 01799 540002) which is a comfortable pub with real ale. However, if you want food with your drink, you need to go about ¼ mile further along the road to the Coach and Horses which, besides a good range of beers, provides excellent meals at an affordable price (telephone: 01799 540292).

THE WALK

NB: If you wish, you can shorten this walk by just over 1¾ miles by continuing on the road at point 7 and picking up the route again at point 10.

Leave the parking area by walking away from the arches along a concrete path. Cross a bridge over the junction of the rivers **Cam** and **Debden Water** to go forward, ignoring a path to the left and passing an odourless sewage works. Go through a gate along a broad lane to reach a wooded area.

The main track goes left but you carry straight on along a narrow path with the wood on your left. Enter woodland and eventually cross a bridge on your right and continue straight ahead, across a field.

Just before reaching the wood, turn left. At first you are walking with the wood on the right. When the wood ends keep going forward along a field to a stile, slightly left, in the fence ahead.

In the summer, the thistles in this area attract large numbers of butterflies and other insects.

Go forward; the path is visible on the ground and will take you to the left edge of woodland ahead. When you reach the wood, **Dean's Grove**, curve with its edge to the right and then leave it to go through a waymarked gap in the left-hand hedge. Now keep the fence to your left. When I was last here there was a group of very beautiful and very friendly horses who were keen to know what I had in my day-bag.

Cross a stile and go forward, keeping the fence on your left. At the corner of the field go through a five-bar gate and turn right to walk beside the fence. Pass a stile on your right but cross the one ahead to enter a drive past a cottage.

At the road turn right for about ¼ mile. This is a busy road so you should keep to the right-hand side. You will descend to a brick bridge, which crosses **Debden Water**. As you climb back up, views of the valley open up to your right. At the top of the hill the road turns sharp right. Here you should cross with care to go left down a path through metal gates.

You are now entering **Debden Park**. Walk downhill with the fence on your right. This is a particularly impressive stretch of parkland with extensive woodland on all sides. Over to the left you can see a Second World War pill box. Pass

Detail of carving on Monk's Barn

between two wooden gateposts and continue forward on a broad cross-field path. After 30 yards or so, look over your left shoulder to see part of a large lake, which up till now has been hidden by trees. Halfway across the field, at a T-junction, turn left to walk across a bridge over a finger of the lake.

Immediately turn right alongside a solid brick barn and walk up the path to enter a churchyard by a metal kissing gate. Go to the right of **Debden church** and leave by the far main gate, across a car park and, at the end of a fence on your right, turn right to walk down a drive. Just before a house turn left to follow a field-edge path and keep with this as it goes right across the field corner through a gap in the

hedge to join a narrow footpath which at first goes right along a field edge but quickly becomes a covered walkway. The route passes through the right-hand side of **Brocton's Plantation**.

You may not see jays here but you are very likely to hear them screeching. For years there have been two folding seats either side of a bench – so far passers-by have observed the request not to remove them.

Later you join the left-hand side of **Spinney Wood** to eventually cross a plank bridge onto the right edge of a field. Just before the end of the field go right over a footbridge to arrive at a field edge. Here go left to reach a lane. You will use a 'permissive path' left by the farmer as he never restores the cross-field path, which should go diagonally left.

 ⑨

At the lane turn right. When you reach a thatched house with a flagpole turn right before it to walk down what is at first a rough lane – this turns into a track that rises up to pass between fields towards woodland. Keep with the track as it twists from one side of the hedge to the other just before the wood.

The first part of this woodland is called Yewtree Plantation but I haven't seen any yew trees here – then again, the next part is called Cabbage Wood and this is made up mainly of oaks.

Keep forward, ignoring side tracks, to pass **Waldegraves Farm** on your right to reach a road.

 ⑩

Turn left then take the track on the right as the road curves round. At a fork you will glimpse a triangulation point on the right-hand track but you keep to the left, with the hedge on your right. Ahead you can see **Newport** with the M11 over in the distance. At the end of this long field go through a gap in the hedge to enter another covered lane, which emerges alongside the active workings of a chalk quarry. Continue on the track, which is now

metalled. Soon after passing **Briar Cottage**, turn left up a white fenced path that brings you onto **Newport Station platform**. Go left over the bridge to cross the line and exit from the station to walk up to the main road.

 ⑪

Turn right to walk along the **High Street** for about ½ mile. This is one of the high spots of the walk. What makes Newport so worthwhile is that nearly all of the buildings along this street, whether they are private or business, old or new, have something of interest about them. Early on you will pass **R & R Saggers** (a rather superior garden centre which specialises in unusual plants). Halfway along you will see the wisteria-covered **Newport House** opposite the wonderful old **Monk's Barn**. Towards the end you will pass the **White Horse** pub and it is worth crossing the road and walking up to **Newport church**, which is surrounded by picturesque buildings. Continue up the main street and, just before you turn off, you will see the **Toll House** with its tariff of charges in old pence ('cow or herd of meat cattle, less than a score: 1d; for every sheep or pig, less than a score: ½d; for every bull: 4d'). Turn right down **Bridge End** then fork right under the railway arch into **Water Lane** to return to your car.

8 | Great Bardfield

The picture postcard village of Finchingfield

The Walk 4½ miles 🕐 3½ hours (allowing time to explore Finchingfield)
Map OS Explorer 195 Braintree & Saffron Walden GR 676305

How to get there

Great Bardfield can be most easily reached by the B1057, which runs between Great Dunmow and the A1017 near Haverhill. Park in the centre of the village near the green, which bears the war memorial.

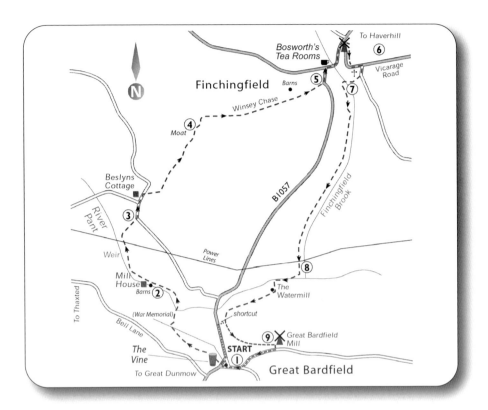

Introduction

Great Bardfield may not be as pretty as the target of this walk, Finchingfield, but it does have a more lived-in feel about it and some stunning buildings. We walk out over meadows to encounter the River Pant and approach Finchingfield with its wonderful old houses, its windmill and what is probably the most photographed and reproduced scene in Essex. The return journey is alongside the cheerfully bubbling Finchingfield Brook. In the course of our stroll we see four mills and enjoy extensive views across the countryside.

Refreshments

The walk starts next to the Vine (telephone: 01371 810355), which provides a good lunch, and there are several other pubs on the walk. However, I recommend that you stop at Bosworth's Tea Rooms in Finchingfield (see point 5).The tea rooms overlook the famous view and seem to offer something to match every appetite and time of day, from breakfasts to cream teas, with a carvery on Sundays (telephone: 01371 810605).

Drive and Stroll

THE WALK

①

Near the war memorial is the **Vine** public house; go to the right of it and walk through the car park and forward, passing the walled beer garden on your left and stables on your right. Go through a metal gate and diagonally left to the corner of the field to a gap. From here go diagonally right to another gap, which provides access to a plank bridge. After crossing, go right along a fenced path. Follow the right-hand fence as it swings to the right to reach a field edge. Go right to follow the edge with the **River Pant** on your right. Just before reaching two corrugated barns, turn right over a footbridge.

②

Turn left to walk alongside the river, across a field boundary, glimpsing **Mill House** through the trees on your left. Go ahead, curving slightly right to reach a stile alongside a weir and water gauging station. Continue along this very pleasant stretch of river bank. Soon after going under power lines, passing a white-railed bridge on your left, cross a stile and turn right to walk up a field edge and reach a lane.

③

Turn left, continuing forward at a junction, and, just after **Beslyns**

Cottage on the left, go right up a track over the brow of a hill. Take a left fork before reaching the hedge ahead. This track takes you along the left edge of a fairly large field. At the field boundary continue forward, but go right of the hedge.

Towards the end of the field, the hedge protrudes to the right – this reflects the position of a moat, which you cannot see but which is sited some 20 yards to the left. Presumably, in the past, this was the site of a large house.

Follow the waymarker which takes you straight across the corner of the field; ahead you can see two large gaps; aim for the left one and cross the ditch by an earth bridge.

④

Turn right along a wide grassy track, which swings left, then right and straightens out to form **Winsey Chase**. Ahead, beyond the terracotta-tiled barn conversions, you can see the tower of **Finchingfield church**. Initially the track has a ditch on the left, later, after a field boundary, you will continue with a hedge on your right. Once you reach the barns the path is enclosed and passes between gardens to eventually go downhill to a road.

⑤

Turn left and walk to a war memorial on a green.

I have been standing on this spot

in the past, seen a coach pull up, its occupants spill out, snap with their cameras, climb back on the coach and be driven away. There is no doubt that the scene ahead of you has most of the elements of the quintessential village view: the green, the duckpond, the attractive houses. The rising ground and the spiralling road up to the church just add to the effect. All that is missing is a couple of carthorses and a few men in smocks.

Over to your left is **Bosworth's Tea Rooms**. Walk over to the **Fox Inn**, crossing the bridge and turning left. Cross the road and join the path on the bank to walk parallel with the road. The scene is dominated by the mill, which we will pass in a few moments. Immediately after **Old Mill Cottage**, turn right to walk along a gravel path.

This is the only surviving member of a group of eight windmills in the parish of Finchingfield. It was probably built in the 1750s. This style of mill, known as a post mill, is the earliest type known in England. The body of the mill contains the machinery and carries the sails. It is balanced upon a large oak post so that it may be turned to face the wind. (It's open to the public on the third Sunday of each month from April to September.

Walk up the path past attractive gardens and continue between houses. Climb a slope, passing an old shed on your right, and emerge on a road opposite the church.

This is the church of St John the Baptist. It is 14th century but with an older Norman tower. There used to be a spire on top of the tower until it blew down during a storm in 1702. The doorway has a fine Norman arch.

Turn left, then right down **Vicarage Road** (wherever you look in this area, there are splendid houses). Just past the church turn right down a road that is forbidden to vehicles of over 3 tons. Follow the curve of the road, then turn left through a squeeze stile to cross a bridge over the **Finchingfield Brook** (noticing the rather superior private bridges both left and right).

Immediately turn left along a fenced path. When the fencing ends, turn right to walk with the brook on your left. You soon join a fence on the right and follow this alongside the brook for over a mile, passing open fields and a couple of large gardens.

A lot of work has been done to build up the bank that you are walking on. This is presumably to stop flooding but, even after heavy rain, I have never seen this particular stream reach a threatening level.

Towards the end of this stretch you are forced away from the brook by a wire fence to find a plank bridge on the left which takes you onto a fenced path. Eventually you reach a farm track with power wires overhead.

Cross the track, slightly to the right, to resume your direction along the left edge of a field. At the end of the field, ignore the footbridge on the left at the corner and carry on around the field edge to reach a smart metal and wood bridge on the left. Cross over and walk ahead to the right of a noisy mill pond.

Cross the bridge between the mill chase and a pond. Here you can experience the power of the water and examine the remains of the waterwheels whose turning drove the mill machinery.

Walk past the restored mill house to turn right opposite stables converted to holiday homes. Keep forward to the right of a line of conifers and continue along the track to turn left over a stile and go along the right edge of a large field.

Ignore a bridge on the right (although you could use this as a short-cut back to the village, turning left when you reach the road). At a waymarked junction, go left to climb up the far edge of the field to the windmill and lane.

This fine tower mill is probably the oldest (c1660) in Essex. It is now privately owned. The fixed tower supports a cap which can be turned, by the fantail, to bring the sails into the wind. The advantage of the Great Bardfield Mill over that at Finchingfield is that it is not necessary to move the whole body of the structure.

Go right to join a lane going downhill. At the bottom go right before a small green and go right up the main road back to the war memorial.

If you are here on a weekday you will see the large model jovial butcher outside the meat shop. On a Sunday it is rather disconcerting to look through the shop window to see him staring out at you.

9 | Halstead

Looking back over the field to Trinity church at the start of the walk

The Walk 4¾ miles 🕐 3 hours
Map OS Explorer 195 Braintree & Saffron Walden GR 810307

How to get there

Halstead is situated on the A131 between Braintree and Sudbury. The Butler Road Car Park is signposted off the High Street at the southern end of the town. There is, indeed, a pay and display car park at the top of Butler Road but if you travel a little further down you will discover ample free parking in a bay nearly opposite our starting point in Beridge Road.

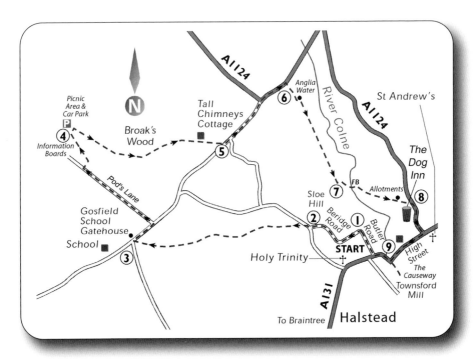

Introduction

Halstead is certainly an attractive town, fascinating to explore and also lovely when seen, as on this walk, from the distance as it nestles between low hills in the Colne Valley. As we leave the town we enter Broak's Wood, an enchanting area that has been effectively opened up for walkers by the Forestry Commission. The return is via a disused railway line and we walk down the High Street before making a short detour to admire a magnificent mill. I have little doubt that you will want to return here – either to shop in the rural atmosphere of a market town or to spend a day further exploring the delights of Broak's Wood.

Refreshments

You will pass the Dog Inn just before you reach the High Street during point 8. The Dog Inn is a wonderful traditional old pub with exposed beams and lots of brass, and, from the back, overlooks the River Colne. It has two bars warmed by open fires in winter. It serves a good selection of real ales and bar meals (telephone: 01787 477774). Possibly more convenient for the finish of the walk is the **Locomotive**, which stands near the top of

Butler Road. This enterprising pub offers breakfast from 9 am, a wide choice of meals at lunchtime and tea or coffee all day (telephone: 01787 472425).

THE WALK

Start the walk by turning down **Beridge Road** on the left off **Butler Road**. Follow this road as it curves right and left to eventually reach a T-junction at **Sloe Hill**.

Cross over and walk a few paces right before turning along a path on the left. This path, with a ditch on the left and a fence on the right, soon delivers you along the lower edge of a field and you continue forward. Cross into the next field alongside a magnificent oak and maintain your direction.

If you look back from here you get an excellent view of Halstead. The elegant spire of Holy Trinity church is particularly prominent and higher up, to the left, you can probably see the tower of St Andrew's.

Halfway along the field, look for a stile on the right – cross it and keep forward to a plank bridge and stile in the corner. Go straight up the hill to enter another field to the right of a redundant stile and continue along the left-hand edge. The descent into a dip brings you to a plank-gate combination, and you

continue, under telephone wires. Continue to a road.

Turn right. Pass the gatehouse of **Gosfield School** and, opposite house numbers 2 and 3, turn left up a track on the edge of woodland. When you reach the end of the field on your right, ignore tracks to left and right to continue forward. Fork left at a junction with a pond on the right. You are now following the broad, ancient **Pod's Lane**. After passing a small pond on the left, look for a waymarker post with a red band. Turn right here to pick up a similar post within 5 yards. Swing left, ignoring a fenced path to the right and continue forward, now on a semi-surfaced footpath. Eventually you reach a car park with an information board.

You have now arrived in a delightful picnic area with log seats as well as the conventional tables and benches. As the board explains, Broak's Wood is owned by the Forestry Commission. It is largely ancient woodland dating from the last Ice Age although, as we have seen, there have been some later plantings. There are over 5 miles of paths in the area and, on a future visit, you may well

Drive and Stroll

Townsford Mill

be content to park here and explore these beautiful woods in greater detail.

 ④

Turn right to walk past the information board to the first of two gates (bearing a 'walkers are welcome' notice) to join a wide track. Keep forward, ignoring side turnings. When you reach a cross-track coming in from the right and going downhill on the left, go left. Keep left when you join a stony track. Eventually views across fields appear on the left and you pass a couple of small ponds on the right to emerge, through a five-bar gate, alongside **Tall Chimneys Cottage** to join its drive and reach a lane.

 ⑤

Turn left and walk along beside some rather fine poplar trees. The lane joins the main road (the A1124) where you turn right. As this is fairly twisty you will need to swap sides to ensure that you are in the view of drivers. After 200 yards you will reach a concrete footpath sign.

 ⑥

Turn right past wire gates to walk along a concrete track. For the next ½ mile you will be walking alongside the track bed of a dismantled railway. Soon you pass a new **Anglia Water installation** and the concrete finishes so you proceed along a broad field-edge path with views of **Halstead** ahead.

If it is a fine day, the poplars over your right shoulder are reminiscent of a Tuscan landscape.

Ignore a turning left at the boundary of the second field and pass the embankment of the Flood Alleviation Scheme, with its dramatically illustrated information board. Continue to the next field boundary with telephone poles coming halfway down; on the left is a stile.

Cross over and, after crossing a second stile, take the middle of three paths on offer. This curves around to the right to accompany a meander of the **River Colne**. Where the path forks, go left alongside the river to cross it by a rather nice metal bridge. Now turn right to walk at first alongside the **Colne** then across the field to woodland, which you skirt to follow the edge of a field to a corner. Keep forward, forking right, up a narrow path, soon passing allotments on your left, then go right to reach a road.

Turn right.

Looking at the housing blocks here, it would seem that someone was an admirer of Jane Austen.

Keep on this road, passing the **Dog Inn** until you reach a mini-roundabout with the **church of St Andrew** opposite. Now turn right past a drinking fountain marking Victoria's Jubilee to walk down the **High Street** – particularly impressive on Sundays when traffic volumes are low. At the bottom of the hill, cross a bridge over a much wider **Colne**.

Turn left down **The Causeway** to visit **Townsford Mill**, which has been converted to an antiques centre and restaurant. Retrace your steps to the main road. You will notice on the left houses with a rather Flemish style of frontage. Go left at the main road and follow this round to turn right on **Butler Road**, passing the **Locomotive** pub and return to your car.

10 Bures

The mill at Bures

The Walk 5 miles or 4 miles if you choose to take the short cut (see map) 🕒3 hours
Map OS Explorer 196 Sudbury, Hadleigh & Dedham Vale GR 908339

How to get there

The village of Bures is roughly halfway along the B1508, which runs between Sudbury and Colchester. Turn off this road into Nayland Road near the church and you will find the car park alongside the village hall on your right.

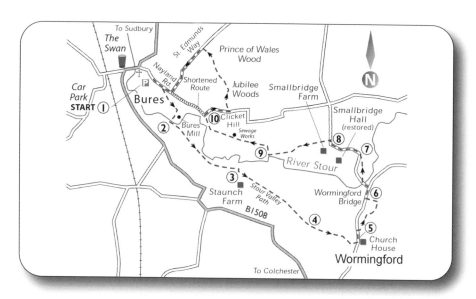

Introduction

A splendid mill, a house where Queen Elizabeth I was entertained, a little climbing to achieve stunning views and the meandering River Stour to keep you company – all this and much more on this walk from **Bures** on the Essex-Suffolk border.

Refreshments

If you walk up from the car park towards the station you will come to two of the three village pubs. The Swan (telephone: 01787 228121) incorporates a bistro which serves a varied range of very good value meals, besides offering sandwiches and snacks. The half-panelled public bar is also worth a visit.

THE WALK

NB: You can shorten this walk by nearly a mile by turning left instead of right at point 10. This will also save you climbing a hill – but you will miss some good views.

Leave the car park and turn right in **Nayland Road** to walk past the village hall and, after a short distance, go right at a footpath sign to go half left across a field. Join a drive and swing left with it through a white gate. Go right with the drive to be confronted with **Bures Mill**. Walk to the right along a track, then over a concrete walkway and right alongside the mill pond.

There has been a mill on this site since 1190; the present one was built in 1640 and extended in 1820. On your right is an unusual automatic anti-flood lock, installed in 1938.

Walk on between white fences to a bridge over a weir.

 ②

Go through a gate. In the field there are two paths, one ahead and one to the left – take the latter along the field edge and head for a stile. Over on your left you can now see the mill, the mill house and the mill pond. Cross the stile and go forward to cross two more stiles. Up to the left you can see the ridge by which we will be returning, with the **Prince of Wales Wood** prominent on the skyline. Cross a plank bridge and across a narrow field to a second footbridge. Go straight ahead, cutting off a corner of the next field before joining its edge. In the next, larger field, continue on a clear cross-field path.

Over to the left is the River Stour. Our outward journey is mainly on the Stour Valley Path.

There are four telegraph poles in this field – after the third pole, turn right with the path up to a gap with **Staunch Farm** ahead.

 ③

Once through the gap turn left. Now you have the hedge on your left and the farm on your right. In the next field go slightly right, aiming for the point where woodland ahead meets a line of isolated trees on the right. Cross a track and continue to the right of the wood, then diagonally left to a gate to the left of an oak tree. Turn right up the fence. When you reach the aptly named '**Fir Trees**' look back for views of your journey – straight ahead in winter you should be able to see **Bures Mill**.

At the top of the hill, leave by a gate slightly left.

 ④

Go forward to another gate secreted in brambles and continue ahead on a path, to the right of a wire fence, which soon descends steeply into a dip and rises through woodland. The path goes left to a kissing gate and into the churchyard at **Wormingford**.

It is always a pleasant surprise to come upon St Andrew's church from this direction. Its tower is Norman but the whole building was overhauled in Victorian times. Inside, a window depicts St George slaying a 'cokadrille', a dragon worm with a girl's legs protruding from its mouth. John Constable's aunt and uncle lived in Wormingford and their tombs can be found in the churchyard.

 ⑤

Leave the churchyard opposite **Church House** by a brick stile and turn left along the road, past the signed footpath to the school, then turn right almost opposite a black barn. The drive leads to a metal gate. Cross the stile on the left. When the drive turns up to a house keep forward past laurels on a narrow path past an old barn and into a strip of woodland to emerge between wire fences onto a track and turn left.

Go right at the road and left when it forks to cross a bridge over the **Stour** (notice the Essex arms carved on its pillars on one side and those of Suffolk on the other). On the other side, enter the field on the right and go diagonally left to a gap with railings just visible where you reach the corner of the road.

Go right to walk along the road with the stables of **Smallbridge Hall** ahead.

There is a public footpath to the left of the drive to the Hall, and I recommend that, as a diversion, you go down this and turn left for a view of the beautifully restored house across its moat. It must look almost the same now as when Sir William Waldegrave entertained Elizabeth I here nearly 400 years ago.

Just past the drive to the Hall go left along a track. When this goes left

continue forward along the field edge to find a metal kissing gate on the left. Go through this to continue your direction, with the hedge now on your right. At the end of the field go left towards a house to go right through a gap and across a concrete path via two seven-bar gates, continuing with the hedge on your right. Continue in the next field and look for another kissing gate on the right near the end.

Go up the field and left along its lower edge. At the far corner go down on a path which takes you past a screened sewage works. Continue forward through a gate and past a plantation of cypress trees to a road.

This is where you can turn left if you wish to shorten the walk by returning to **Bures** along the road.

For the main route, turn right up **Clicket Hill**. At the top turn left along a farm track. The walk now takes on an almost regal tone as we pass **Jubilee Wood**, its **Golden Jubilee** extension and eventually **Prince of Wales Wood** – all with suitable identification plaques. About 300 yards after passing a barn with a small pond, at a concrete cross-track, turn left to descend to a housing estate alongside which you continue to the main road and turn right to return to the car park.

11 | Chappel

Views of the viaduct dominate the last mile or so of the walk

The Walk 6 miles ⏱ 4 hours
Map OS Explorer 195 Basildon & Saffron Walden and 184 Colchester (mainly) GR 897288

How to get there

Chappel is halfway along the A1124, which runs between the A131 at Halstead and the A12 west of Colchester. Turn north at the road by the viaduct (signed to the station) and soon turn right up the station approach. There is free parking outside the station and a large overflow area in a field. There are toilets (preserved in their original state!) on the station platform.

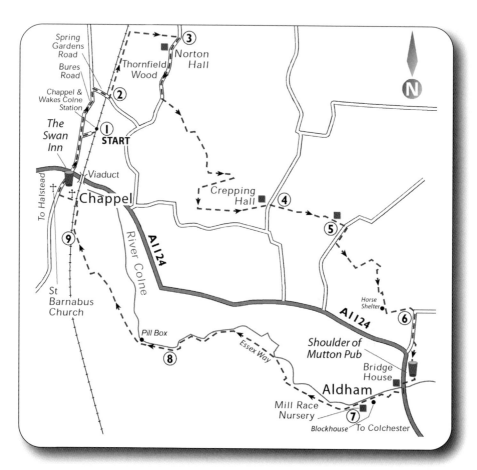

Introduction

From the railway museum at Chappel this varied walk takes you first through attractive woodland and then over open landscapes with wide views before descending to pick up the River Colne as it winds its erratic way back to the village. Whilst the beauty of the river and the buildings associated with it will no doubt impress, especially at Aldham, it will be the encounter with the viaduct at the end of the route that is likely to be most memorable.

Refreshments

For a cup of tea or coffee and a biscuit or two there is the café in the visitors' centre at the station. If you want a drink on the walk, the Shoulder of Mutton is situated at Aldham, a little over halfway round the route. However, if you

Drive and Stroll

can contain your appetite until the end, then I recommend the Swan Inn at Chappel – especially if you like fish and real ale (telephone: 01787 222353).

THE WALK

Walk back down from the station to the road and turn right up **Bures Road**. After ¼ mile turn right down **Spring Gardens Road** and cross the bridge.

Looking to the right you get a good view of the station and some of the exhibits of the museum. Note that this is a single track railway, relatively uncommon in this part of the world. Commuters can use the hourly service to Marks Tey and then catch trains to Colchester or London.

On the other side of the bridge go left to walk along the left edge of the field parallel with the railway track. Continue on the left-hand side of the next field and, at the corner, go diagonally right on a narrow path to a waymarker which takes you left along an attractive woodland path. When you are nearly at the end of the wood turn right, away from the railway, and walk along just inside the trees until you emerge by a gate to continue up the left side of a field to a lane.

Turn right. On the right are the attractive gardens of **Norton Hall** and, ahead, views over the **Colne Valley**. The lane descends to a railed bridge. Just after crossing this turn left at a concrete finger-post to walk along a field with a stream and a hedge on your left. At the field's end cross a footbridge, which is tucked away in a corner. Go forward for about 10 yards, then turn right through a gate over an earth bridge to walk along with a hedge on your left to another earth bridge and continue to the end of a second field. Here go left up a broad track soon between wicket fencing. You reach a small clearing – do not go forward but turn right through almost 180 to go down another broad track. At the bottom, cross a stile by a green gate and turn left going along the left field edge. At a second field boundary, turn left to cross a footbridge, continuing up a path to go forward across a field and left of a patch of scrub. As you gain height houses come into view and you should aim to go right of an evergreen hedge ahead; this leads you to a stile. Once over, walk with a wooden fence on your left, and when this turns away keep forward across the field to a stile beside a gate. Go straight across the lane.

Over on the left you will see Crepping Hall with some cleverly restored farm buildings.

 ④

Walk up the right side of a field. You are now on a ridge with good views to the right and lots of sky if it's a sunny day. At the end of the field go alongside a newly laid out garden and join a drive.

On the skyline ahead you will notice the tower of the church of St Mary which stands some distance away from its village of West Bergholt, alongside the local hall.

 ⑤

When you reach the road turn right and, after a few yards, go left of the hedge and continue along the right edge of the field. On reaching the corner go left and do the same at the next. On the third side ignore a wide signed gap to later cross a footbridge with a metal rail on the right. Go right through trees and up a flight of steps to a gate. Turn right along the field edge. At the end go slightly left through a gate over a bridge and continue on the right side of the next field. Swing left just before reaching a horse shelter to pick up a shingle track which you follow out of the field to a road.

 ⑥

Turn right (if it is clear, there is a path to the right of the hedge which is preferable to walking along the road). Whichever way you go, continue until you reach a concrete finger-post taking you left over a plank bridge and along the right edge of a field. Cross into a second field and keep going with houses on the right, and when these finish look for a narrow path on the right (if you see the river, you have probably passed it). The path takes you down by the side of the river, over a bridge and up into the car park of the **Shoulder of Mutton** pub.

Cross the road and turn left over the bridge. (Here you will see the sign announcing **Aldham**, although, from the map, you may imagine that you are still in **Fordstreet**.) It is worth pausing here for a few minutes to briefly take in the view of the outskirts of **Aldham**. Once over the bridge pass the drive to **Bridge House** and immediately turn right between a garage and a chain fence, which develops into a magnificent wall and a white wooden fence. Cross a gap and continue on a narrow path between a wooden fence and a privet hedge on the right. Here you get glimpses of delightful gardens and after crossing a bridge reach an attractive section of the **River Colne**. Soon you are walking alongside the giant **Mill Race Nursery**. At a picnic area make for the right-hand side of a Second World War pill box.

In the summer time, especially at weekends, you can hire rowing boats here.

Now you keep to the field edge on your right avoiding, if it is early summer, the temptation of the mass of strawberries and raspberries to your left.

 ⑦

At the end of the nursery boundary go forward along the edge of a mile-long field. Towards the end of the field you rejoin the **Colne** to mimic its meanders for a few minutes until you reach a bridge tucked away in a corner on your right.

 ⑧

Go ahead with the river on your right to pass a brick bridge and go through a gate by a pill box. Now keep to the left of wire fences for two fields. In the third field, continue with a hedge to your right. Where the hedge ends, keep forward across the field to a waymarker. From this, go diagonally left to another waymarker and along the fence to the end of the field. Go left to join a lane. Climb the bank on the right by a waymarker. Set out across the field, aiming for the left-hand corner.

 ⑨

Follow another waymarker over a bridge and turn right. After crossing a stile you emerge under the wonderful viaduct.

You will have been getting glimpses of the viaduct for over a mile now but nothing quite prepares you for the close-up experience. There is a beauty about the workmanship and design that is regrettably rarely matched in today's utilitarian structures. The most astonishing sight is when you look to your right through the centre of the arches and at a remarkable pattern of brickwork – I have come across people who have been here many times and never noticed this.

Turn left along a broad track, under the viaduct (this is where you should look right) and walk up to the road.

This presents another delightful scene with the white, wooden-spired church of St Barnabas, a green and several attractive buildings set out before you.

Turn right to walk up the road and past the **Swan Inn**, across the **Colne** for the last time, crossing the main road and continuing up **Station Road** to go right to return to your car.

12 Manningtree

Flatford Mill

The Walk 4½ miles   🕐 3½ hours (allowing time to linger at Flatford Mill)

Map OS Explorer 196 Sudbury, Hadleigh & Dedham Vale GR 094322

How to get there

Try to avoid approaching from Colchester. It is best to take a turning off the A12 (north of Colchester) to Dedham. This will give you the bonus of driving up Dedham High Street and glimpsing the church. On the outskirts of Manningtree, which is signed from Dedham, take the turning to the station. Here you will find two massive pay & display car parks. The cost of parking is reduced after 9.30 am and at weekends. **Alternatively**, if you don't fancy paying parking fees, you could start from the car park outside Lawford church, at point 2.

Drive and Stroll

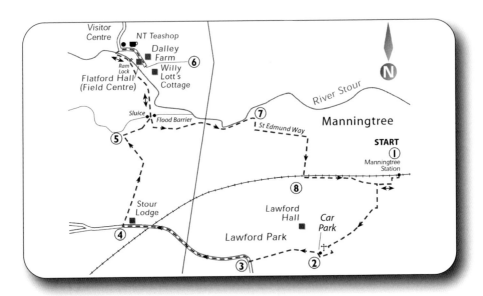

Introduction

Flatford Mill on the River Stour was the first home of the Constable Family. John Constable's brother went to live there after their father's death and John was a frequent visitor. Living in the area and going to school in nearby Dedham it is hardly surprising that one of England's most famous painters should have used what he saw as the basis of his early paintings.

On this walk you will see Dedham church in the distance in much the same way as Constable saw it. If you know *The Mill Stream* you should have little trouble recognising the scene when you reach Flatford Mill, although he used a little more artistic licence in his better-known *The Hay Wain*, which was inspired by the same view. To reach the mill the walk first rises to the side of the valley where you will encounter a lovely old church and an imposing manor. You will return along the Stour flood plain to discover the hidden delights of the station at **Manningtree**.

Refreshments

You can get an excellent cup of tea at the National Trust Tea Rooms at Flatford Mill. Here there is the characteristically wide range of home-made cakes, which supplement the delicious light lunches. However, the main reason for starting the walk from Manningtree Station is to persuade you to try a breakfast at the Station Buffet on the platform here which is open from 5.30 am till 9 pm on weekdays. The Buffet, which is a favourite with walkers, besides serving a wide range of snacks and meals also has a well-stocked bar, featuring at least four real ales (telephone: 01206 391114).

THE WALK

From the station, turn right and walk down a ramp. Turn left across the entrance to the lower car park and continue down a short footpath to turn right along a wide track. After just 40 yards turn left up a footpath signposted to **Lawford**. As you walk up the hill you begin to get good views over the **Stour Estuary** to your left. Halfway up the hill, swing right, then left to skirt a plantation.

On your right is a good example of a laid hedge that clearly displays the intricate structure which, by partially cutting and laying the main trees, ensures that later shoots can grow vertically and be pegged in. Hedges of this kind mature into a barrier that is impenetrable to animals.

At the very top the laid hedge gives way to a wire fence on the right. Continue as the path narrows to pass a graveyard on the left and eventually enter a churchyard. Go left, then right at a cross to pass the front of the church.

It is thought that a church has existed on this site since Saxon times. The present St Mary's, the parish church of Lawford, was built by the Lord of the Manor in 1340. This explains why it is considerably nearer to his home, Lawford Park, which you will see in a few moments, than the homes of the parishioners. One of the most striking aspects is the chequerboard pattern using dressed flint – it is thought to be one of the best examples of the Decorated style in Essex.

Leave by the main entrance.

Cross to the right-hand corner of the car park and go through a kissing gate, then go slightly right across the field to another gate. Turn left on the drive (**Lawford Park** is over to the far right) and continue to a road.

Turn right and follow the road down, under power lines and a railway bridge, to climb up again and, after about 200 yards, turn right immediately after a house to a gate set back from the road.

Cross a stile incorporated into a gate and descend into the **Stour Valley** by a broad grassy track (over to the left you can see **Dedham church**). At the very bottom, go left, then right to cross a stile and bridge combination with a National Trust sign. Go forward parallel to the hedge on the right, swinging slightly left toward the end. Cross a metal-railed bridge. Continue across the next field towards its far left corner where you come to a cross-track.

Go right on the track to cross a concrete bridge by a metal kissing gate. Now go ahead to a second kissing gate and walk alongside a flood barrier, passing a sluice gate on your right. Continue on a raised path (the area each side is a nature reserve) to eventually bear left with a wall, which borders the mill pond of **Flatford**. Continue past a weir and lock to turn right to cross a bridge over the **Stour**.

Slightly left is a visitor centre, along to the right is a National Trust teashop and you can walk further along to view the other side of Flatford Mill and Willy Lott's Cottage. Don't miss the spectacular Valley Farm on the left. It is appropriate that painting courses can be taken in the study centre now housed in the mill. Besides enjoying the beautiful buildings and the stunning setting you can rest on one of the numerous seats or, if you feel more energetic, hire a rowing boat or join a guided tour. If you have no bread for the ducks you can buy some from the visitors' centre.

When you have exhausted all possibilities, retrace your steps by crossing the bridge and turning left. On reaching the flood barrier, walk alongside it and turn left at the very end. This path, which is on top of an earth wall, goes through two gates and, after passing under power lines, follows the course of the **Stour** fairly closely. After the river completes a particularly exaggerated meander you go through a gate and immediately turn right at a signpost to **Manningtree Station**.

Go through another gate to join a broad hedged track, which soon swings left. After ¼ mile the track goes right and continues ahead to pass under a railway bridge.

Turn left to walk parallel with the railway on your left until you reach a waymarker on the left, which takes you back to the station.

13 | Coggeshall Hamlet

Willows and bridges are features of this walk

The Walk 4½ miles 🕐 2½ hours
Map OS Explorer 195 Braintree & Saffron Walden GR 852216

How to get there

Coggeshall Hamlet is on a minor road that runs between Kelvedon and Coggeshall off the B1024. You will approach it either by the A120 from Braintree or the A12 from Chelmsford. Once you reach the hamlet, look for a row of houses set back off the road on the eastern side – you can park on a gravelled area in front of them. **Alternatively** you could start the walk in Coggeshall. There is a free car park near the library mentioned in point 7 (off Stoneham Street).

Drive and Stroll

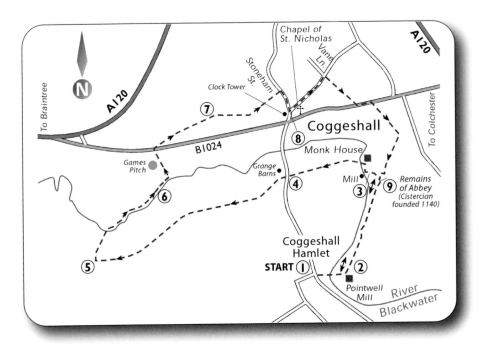

Introduction

There are few walking experiences to match passing along a lazily flowing river with lines of green weed weaving in and out of the currents. Add some weeping willows, bridges, weirs and a water mill or two and you have one of the pleasantest strolls in Essex. Besides taking you through the ancient complex of what remains of an old abbey I couldn't resist introducing some of the gems of Coggeshall itself.

This walk from **Coggeshall Hamlet** will be interesting at any time of the year but will be best done in late spring or summer. At these times the trees will be displaying their elegant foliage, it will be drier underfoot and the fascinating 12th century Grange Barn will be open to visitors.

I think that the start of the route is so beautiful that I have purposely repeated it at the end.

Refreshments

During the walk, at the end of point 7 in Stoneham Street, you will pass the spectacular Clock Tower Tea Rooms (telephone: 01376 563242), which specialises in home-made cakes and cream teas along with old-fashioned puddings and traditional Welsh rarebit. For a more substantial meal I recommend the pub next door – the Chapel Inn which has a wide-ranging menu which can be accompanied by a grand selection of real ales (telephone: 01376 561655).

THE WALK

NB: If you wanted to drastically shorten the walk you could return back along the road from **Grange Barn** (point 4) to your car.

Walk up to the road from the parking area and turn left. Almost immediately, turn left down **Pointwell Lane**. You are immediately in an area of well-kept and individual houses and gardens.

At the end of the lane go forward through a gate, over a cattle grid and alongside a beautifully converted mill with a pond on your right. Turn left to walk to a wide bridge and pass under a weeping willow. Now proceed along the river bank.

This stretch of riverside walking along the Blackwater is as good as anything you are likely to experience in Essex. It is particularly fine in the spring and summer when the willows on the opposite bank are just touching the water.

Cross a bridge over a weir, keep to the river edge and, at the end of a field go over a high stile and follow the river round to the left to join a track.

Cross the river and mill pond.

Stop on the second bridge for excellent views to either side. To your left is another mill and to the right you can see part of Monk House. If there is little or no breeze and the water is still the reflections can be memorable.

Go right at the farmyard.

On your left are some stables and on your right you will see the remains of a Cistercian Abbey founded in 1140.

Follow the track round to the left.

Over your right shoulder is the front of Monk House, a 16th century farmhouse which is a private residence and not open to the public.

Where another lane comes in from the left, keep forward.

Just beyond this junction, on the right-hand side, is the gatehouse chapel of St Nicholas, the most complete of the abbey buildings,

Monk House

which was built about 1220. *Locally made bricks were used in its construction and it is the earliest post-Roman brickwork in England. Halfway up this wider lane you can see the town of Coggeshall over on the right.*

 ④

Go across the road, passing **Grange Barn**.

This barn was also originally part of the Cistercian abbey. It is the oldest surviving timber-framed barn in Europe and dates from around 1140. The roof would have originally been thatched but was replaced with tiles around the 14th century. Now owned by the National Trust, it contains a collection of farm carts and wagons and is open to the public from the end of March to mid October from 2 pm till 5 pm on Tuesdays, Thursdays and Sundays.

Just after the barn, notice an old-fashioned petrol pump on the right. Continue past a metal barn on the left and along the track, part of the **Essex Way**, for about a mile. Partway along the track swings to the other side of the hedge.

 ⑤

When this hedge on the right ends, turn right to walk down the field edge with a ditch on your right towards woodland. Cross a bridge into a plantation of willows and go forward following the path on the ground to eventually cross an elegant green metal footbridge and turn right. Follow the meanders of the **River Blackwater** for about ¼ mile.

The path eventually swings away from the river and climbs a slope. Keep forward, with a games pitch to the left. Continue and go through a car park to reach the main road. Go diagonally right across the road to a concrete finger-post and join a field-edge path, with buildings on your right. Continue through a kissing gate then, at a corner, keep ahead under laurels to cross a narrow drive, then go straight across a field to a waymarker by a chestnut tree.

Turn slightly right to keep to the right-hand edge of this next field, aiming for a solid wooden fence. At the crossing of the tracks, take the surfaced path forward with the fence on your right. Cross a bridge to arrive at a road with **Millennium Gardens** on your right. Go left and right to reach a road by a library. Turn right here and walk to the major junction. Over to the right is the **Clock Tower Tea Rooms**, a good place to pause awhile.

Turn left along the road signed to **Earls Colne**.

This short stroll brings in a number of fine buildings; many have beams with a thin wash returning them to their original appearance.

When you see **Vane Lane** on the left, turn right down a narrow, walled alley to go over a recreation ground and reach a road. Cross the road and turn left. Just past a line of houses turn right onto a field-edge path and go forward through a metal kissing-gate to proceed with trees on your right. About a quarter of the way along this field you may see a spring emerging by the field path. Cross a concrete track at the corner and enter a third field, now with a stream on your right. Just before the next field edge, go right on a track for 4 yards, then turn left with the hedge on your left and the river coming in from your right.

You should now recognise where you are – this was part of your outward route. Cross the stile, then go over the bridge and across the weir to reach the wide willow-bedecked bridge before the mill. Go forward, then right by the yellow-painted mill, out through the gate, up the lane and turn right at the road to return to your parking place.

14 Mersea

Looking across Pyefleet Channel

The Walk 5¼ miles 🕐 3 hours
Map OS Explorer 184 Colchester GR 064145

How to get there

Take the B1025 south out of Colchester for about 6 miles until you come onto Mersea Island. Take the left fork and follow the road for nearly 3 miles. Just after passing the Dog and Pheasant on the left go forward on a corner along a narrow lane signposted to the Cudmore Grove Country Park car park. This is a pay and display car park with a visitor centre and toilets. **Alternatively** if you would prefer not to pay for parking you could continue to the end of the 'main' road where you will find a small car park. Parking here will mean that you join the walk at point 2.

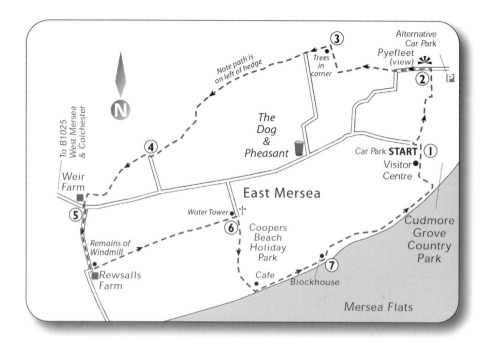

Introduction

You are likely to experience a slight frisson of excitement as you drive across the causeway to **Mersea** on the first occasion. Warning notices asking you to take extra care if the road is covered with water don't help. In reality the Strood, as the causeway is called, is only flooded at spring tides when the route is unsafe for about an hour.

Mersea is England's most easterly inhabited island. In fact most of the people live in West Mersea, where you can find all the bustle and hustle of a busy holiday resort. East Mersea, where we are walking, is rather bleaker – providing more opportunities to observe wildlife attracted by the salt marshes and with uninterrupted views out to sea and across to the mainland.

Refreshments

At weekends you can buy drinks and ice creams at the Park visitor centre. There is also a pub, the Dog and Pheasant (telephone: 01206 383206), near the start of the walk. On the other side of the island, in West Mersea, the West Mersea Oyster Bar (telephone: 01206 381600) is a fabulous and reasonably-priced fish restaurant at the northern end of the coast road but it can be difficult to park near there during summer weekends.

Drive and Stroll

THE WALK

Walk away from the visitor centre to the car park entrance. Just past the start of the one-way system, turn right to go down a bank and cross a footbridge which takes you to a drive. Turn right and follow the drive uphill, taking a left fork just before houses. Continue forward with a wire fence on the left and a hedge on your right. Just before a five-bar gate, turn right and follow a fenced path as it goes around the edge of a field.

To your right, through the trees, you can see across the Colne Estuary (the Brightlingsea Reach) to Brightlingsea and St Osyth.

At the end of the field you reach a road.

Turn left to walk along with houses on the right (a quick diversion on the right to see **Pyefleet View** is worthwhile). Where the row of houses ends, the road turns sharp left but you go forward, slightly right, to walk up a signposted track to cross a stile to the left. A sequence of three more stiles brings you to a field edge. Keep to the hedge on the left, and when this ends by a water trough keep forward across the field.

Now, over to the right, you can see the Pyefleet Channel with Rat Island to the right and Fingringhoe Ranges to the left. There is no access to the ranges as they are used for live firing but the site does house a nature reserve.

Soon you will see a stile in the hedge ahead of you. When you reach the stile do not cross it but turn right and go over the field to the right of trees in the far left-hand corner. Here you will find a stile that gives access to a track.

Walk to the left up the track and keep forward when a drive joins from the right. The track, which is now surfaced, turns sharply left but you go forward along the left edge of a field. When the hedge on your left turns away, keep forward across the middle of the field to pick up a hedge on the other side (now on your right). At the field corner, find and go through a kissing gate and across a plank bridge to continue with the hedge on your right. Cross two bridges at the end of the next field and continue with a ditch on your right to reach a fourth field which is larger than the others. You again continue along the right-hand edge, following its curving boundaries first left and then right to eventually join a wide green track, which narrows to bring you onto a lane.

The smart walkway where you join the sea wall

 ④

Turn right and after about 15 yards left to go along the edge of a field with a ditch on your left. At the field boundary keep forward across a bridge and go left at a corner, still keeping the ditch on your left. Ignore a large gap on the left but, just after this, when the hedge swings left, carry on diagonally right across the field to the right of a tree on the corner of the hedge, which you walk along for a short distance to cross a stile. Turn left to walk between the buildings of **Weir Farm** and reach a road.

⑤

Turn left and almost immediately right down a lane signposted to the Mersea Vineyard. After about ¼ mile you reach the rather grand **Rewsalls Farm** with the remains of a small wind generator to the left of it. At the farm entrance turn left to take a track across fields.

To your right you have views of the open sea and ahead, your immediate target, is the parish church of East Mersea. This church may be of particular interest to some as, in the Schools' Mathematics Project (SMP) of the 70s, the churches of Mersea were featured as a means of teaching the rudiments of elevation and bearings. As you draw nearer you will also observe an unusual small water tower alongside less interesting tanks.

You arrive at a road with the church on the opposite side.

Turn right to walk through the entrance to **Coopers Beach Holiday Park**. Go past reception and, where the park's drive curves left, carry straight on past a metal gate. The path swings left past a rather superior children's play area and you continue halfway up a slipway. Turn left to pass a café, an amusement arcade and a swimming pool, then join a rough path that develops into a smart promenade along the sea wall.

If you are an aficionado of caravan styles you will find the selection on the left interesting, ranging as they do through Tudor and Georgian with some clearly modelled on the maritime. To your right you have the open sea and, if it is low tide and depending on the time of the year, the opportunity to view thousands of birds feeding. Men

digging for bait worms can usually be seen on the mud flats and, if you are lucky, sailing barges with their reddish-brown sails out to sea.

Shortly after passing a pill box the path turns inwards and the concrete surface goes. Now turn right and walk along the grassy top of the rather less substantial sea wall. Soon you will encounter more caravans on your left; this is the Fen Farm Park. Now you continue forward along the spring tide level, with a vast number of shells crunching underfoot. Just as the caravans finish on your left, step across a small stream in the shingle and walk along to the right of a low cliff with a mass of groynes ahead. Just after passing the first line of these short posts go left on a steep path up the cliff (the 300,000-year-old bones of a monkey and the remains of a hippopotamus have been found here). At the top go through a fence to a path and at a T-junction turn left, then right. Ahead you will see the visitor centre and car park.

15 | Tollesbury Wick Marshes

The marina packed with yachts

The Walk 5 miles ⏱3 hours
Map OS Explorer 176 Blackwater Estuary GR 963105

How to get there

From the A12 take the B1019 through Hatfield Peverel and skirt Maldon to join the B1026, turning right on the B1023 at Tolleshunt D'Arcy. When you reach Tollesbury, drive through the village and look for Woodrolfe Road on the left. The Woodrolfe Green car park, which has toilets, is about ¼ mile down the road on the left-hand side.

Drive and Stroll

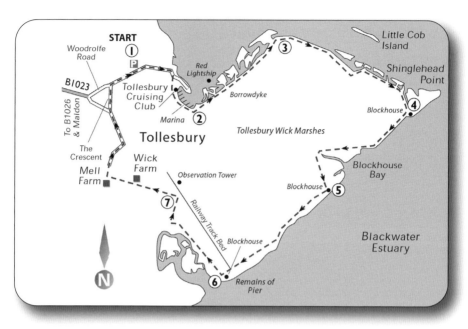

Introduction

Tollesbury is a bustling village off the B1026, east of Maldon. The walk skirts **Tollesbury Wick Marshes** using the sea wall. The route is very easy to follow and, on a clear day, you can see over to Mersea Island and the huge nuclear power station of Bradwell on the other side of the Blackwater Estuary.

However, views are not the main reason for taking this walk. It encircles 600 acres of marshland that, together with the foreshore, form a Site of Special Scientific Interest (SSSI). On the marsh you will see flocks of grazing geese, hear skylarks and glimpse birds of prey, whilst there are many kinds of gull and waders on the mud and salt marsh outside the wall. The marshes were originally reclaimed from the sea in the late Middle Ages but even before that there is evidence of Romans having used pools in the area to obtain salt. More recent activity has resulted in blockhouses and an observation post built as part of the Second World War defence of the estuary.

Make sure you have your binoculars with you on this walk.

Refreshments

You will find the King's Head pub (telephone: 01621 869203) in the attractive square near the church. Although it stocks an excellent range of real ales it sells no food. Across the road, though, is the post office, which is open seven days a week, and sells freshly-cut sandwiches and baguettes.

THE WALK

Leave the car park and turn left to walk down the road. When you reach wooden-clad houses (sail lofts) and boats on the left the roads swings right; just before this follow the footpath sign up steps on the right to a bank and follow the path. With the marina packed with yachts on your left go past **Tollesbury Cruising Club** on the right.

Swing left and enter the nature reserve, now with a twin wire fence on your left, and continue to skirt the marina. Go through a gate with a nature reserve information point to walk along the sea wall, initially with **Mersea Island** ahead, a red lightship on the left, and a water channel on your right.

This water channel, or borrowdyke, was created during the construction of the sea wall and provides the bonus of an additional environment so that you can observe ducks, geese and swans on your right and oystercatchers, terns and many other waders on your left. This stretch of the mud flats also features many small boats in varying stages of decomposition.

After about ½ mile the path goes at right-angles towards the **Blackwater Estuary**. Now, if the visibility is at all reasonable, you will see ahead the vast bulk of the **Bradwell Nuclear Power Station** on the other side of the estuary.

Go forward for another ½ mile, passing mud flats and the two **Cob Islands** on your left. Eventually you will reach **Shinglehead Point** with its Second World War blockhouse.

You now turn right to walk with the estuary on your left. The sea wall turns inland then comes out again around **Blockhouse Bay**. Another blockhouse is sited where it resumes its original direction.

A further ½ mile brings you to a final blockhouse, which is down on the shore and an interpretation panel.

If you look right opposite the blockhouse you will see a slightly raised bank that travels up to the left of an observation tower in the distance. This is the track bed of the Tollesbury Light Railway, which was opened in 1904 as a Victorian attempt to turn the area into another Southend by building a

Drive and Stroll

The marshes

railway out to a pier. Although you can still see the foundations of the pier to your left, the pier deck was removed in 1940 to prevent the possibility of an invading army using it for a landing. The line itself was closed in 1951 and two years later work started on a new sea wall following floods. You can appreciate the increase in height by comparing the present wall with the track bed.

 ⑥

Just beyond the blockhouse you turn sharply inland, parallel to the route of the light railway on your right. After you go through a metal gate the path curves to the left and, after about 30 yards, you should turn right to walk up the left of a field along a hedged path.

 ⑦

Where you meet a cross-track (with a wartime observation post ahead), turn left and go forward passing two farms and then turn right into a lane. Soon there are houses on both sides. Follow the road until you reach **Crescent Road** (opposite 32 & 34 on the right) where you turn right. Follow this to **Woodrolfe Road** and turn right to return to the car park.

16 | Maldon

The Chelmer Blackwater navigation

The Walk 3 miles ⏲ 2½ hours
Map OS Explorer 183 Chelmsford & The Rodings GR 853071

How to get there

Maldon is best reached by taking the A414 from the A12 outside Chelmsford. Follow this road through Danbury and eventually go right following signs to Maldon's town centre, which will bring you into the High Street. To reach the pay and display car park turn down Butt Lane by the Rose and Crown.

Drive and Stroll

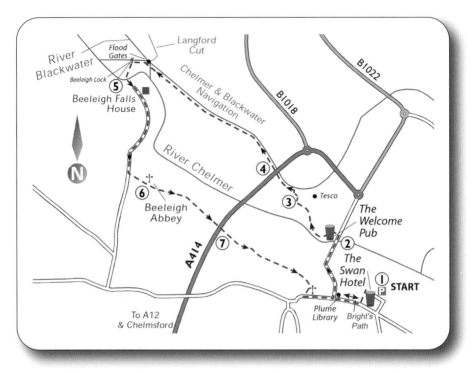

Introduction

Starting and finishing through the historic port of **Maldon**, this route is packed with variety. You will stroll along a particularly peaceful section of the Chelmer and Blackwater Navigation and cross over the dramatic confluence of four distinct waterways. On your return along attractive covered paths and through meadows you will come across the visual delights of Beeleigh Falls House and its neighbouring abbey.

This is a walk that is best done when the ground is fairly dry. Don't forget your camera!

Refreshments

Near the end of the walk you will pass the Bakers Oven on the right of the High Street. This is excellent for a cup of coffee and freshly-filled baguettes. Further on, nearly opposite The Moot Hall in Kings Courtyard is the Courtyard Café for more substantial fare, which on warm days can be served outside. Neither of these is open on Sundays. If you fancy a pub, the Swan Hotel provides good value simple meals and real ales. It is situated alongside the pedestrian exit of the car park in the High Street (telephone: 01621 853170).

THE WALK

Walk out of the car park, past the **Swan Hotel**, to the **High Street** and turn right. Pass **Bright's Path** and, at the tower of the **Plume Library** turn right.

Thomas Plume paid for the demolition of St Peter's church and for its reconstruction as a library room over a schoolroom in 1697. The tower of the old church was rebuilt in traditional Gothic style. Its principal collection consists of a wide range of 16th and 17th century British and European publications with emphasis on theology, history and natural philosophy. The Maeldune Heritage Centre is housed in the same building.

The walk down the hill reveals a whole range of styles in housing from the aged to the sensitively developed to the downright eccentric – particularly the lighthouse-like building at the bottom of the hill. Cross the river.

Turn left to pass immediately to the right of the **Welcome** pub, walk through a small housing development and go left up a

slope, through barriers, to join a surfaced path that borders the river on your left.

Just after passing **Tesco's car park**, turn right and immediately left on duck boards amongst reeds. Fork right and go left when you reach the river edge. If all has gone well you should be walking alongside the **Chelmer and Blackwater Navigation** on your right. You next pass under the A414.

Continue, passing a fine brick-built bridge. Here the **Navigation** is wider and there is a golf course on your left. Eventually the path joins the drive to the clubhouse. The drive takes you to a bridge, which you do not cross.

To the right of this bridge are what, at first glance, appear to be lock gates. These are in fact flood gates, which enable water to be controlled to prevent the flooding of Heybridge further down.

Go forward past the bridge to cross a wooden-railed footbridge over a weir and, just before reaching the lock, turn left down a narrow path.

This whole area is quite remarkable

in terms of water management because here you have the confluence of four distinct waterways: the River Chelmer, the River Blackwater, the Chelmer and Blackwater Navigation and the Langford Cut. To further complicate matters, this is a place where salt water meets fresh, with rich consequences for the diversity of flora and fauna. The Beeleigh Lock (which you will see but not pass) is the first of 14 on the Chelmer and Blackwater Navigation, which is a canal, built in the 1790s to carry goods the 14 miles from the Blackwater Estuary to Chelmsford.

Go across a couple of small bridges before swinging left over a longer wooden footbridge. Cross another small bridge and go through a metal kissing gate to walk to the right of the remains of a mill and **Beeleigh Falls House**. Over the next ¼ mile the drive to the house gradually becomes a lane. Look for a signposted footpath up a drive on your left. Soon you will pass **Beeleigh Abbey** on the left.

The abbey was established in 1119 and dissolved in 1596. Its remains

are now privately owned and there is no public admission. However, from the path you can get a good view of the picturesque farmhouse, which was built in about 1570.

Continue on a fine little path, which meanders through narrow meadows. Just as a bridge at **Maldon** comes into view there is a fork. Go right to find a stile and walk up a tree-covered path, which leads you to another stile at the edge of the A414.

Cross with extreme care to the flight of steps opposite. After crossing the stile at the top onto another covered footpath you come to an area on your right that would be very suitable for a picnic. Keep on forward and when another drive crosses, go slightly left between fences. This path loses height and eventually joins a road. Continue ahead until, after passing **Maldon Court School**, you swing gently right past the parish church to turn left into the **High Street**. Keep along this until you reach the pedestrian access to the car park.

17 | Mill Green

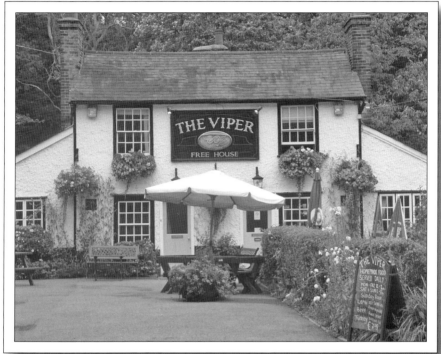

The unique Viper

The Walk 3¾ miles ⏱ 2½ hours
Map OS Explorer 183 Chelmsford & The Rodings GR 637013

How to get there

You can reach Mill Green from the A414 west of Chelmsford but the easiest way is to turn off the A12 to Ingatestone and look for a turning off the main road (the B1002) to Fryerning – this is easy to miss as it is narrow at the start and has stone bollards on each side. Once you reach Fryerning, Mill Green is signposted. The car park is on the common, nearly opposite the Cricketers public house.

Drive and Stroll

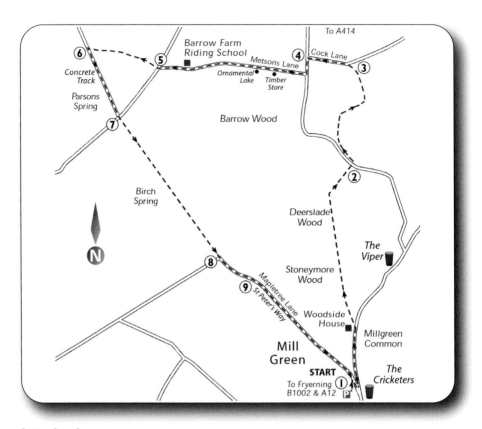

Introduction

This is a woodland walk to the north of **Mill Green**. It starts on Millgreen Common – which has a fascinating history – and then tours four contrasting woods, which have something special to offer at any time of year. You have the chance to see the area's vast range of wood products at close quarters and may even catch fleeting glimpses of deer.

Refreshments

In addition to the Cricketers (telephone: 01277 352400), which is opposite the car park, there is an interesting pub reached by driving ½ mile along Mill Green Road. **The Viper** (telephone: 01277 352010), the only pub in the country with this name, is a traditional inn. The beer is excellent and the food satisfying. If you visit in the summer you will have the bonus of a wonderful display of hanging baskets.

THE WALK

Before you start your walk, it is worth examining the superbly produced information boards on the edge of the car park. When you are ready, leave by the far end of the car park, to the left of the boards, along a grassy track. Go slightly left to reach a drive and turn right to the road. Turn left and just after passing **Woodside House**, go left on a bridleway. Keep ahead, ignoring all tempting side paths and passing 'Private – keep to the bridlepath' notices on your right, to go gradually downhill through rich mixed woodland.

After a second dip the track rises gently to go very slightly right at a white-topped marker post, which brings you to a field edge. Go straight across the field to reach a lane.

Cross over and go left on the other side of the hedge. Follow the edge of a substantial field, always with the hedge on your left, passing a white-topped marker post to eventually come to a T-junction, with a wood ahead. Turn left to walk down the edge of the wood.

Join a drive between houses and cross a stream. At an old-fashioned (but, I suspect, not genuine) lamp post go left. Eventually you will reach a road.

Turn left, then soon right down **Metsons Lane**.

At first you may think that you have entered a timber merchant's yard. More accurately, the timber merchant's wares have spilled out into the lane, providing you with a rare and interesting opportunity to examine how the product of the local woodland is used. Here you will see all the conventional material for fencing and building sheds and will probably be amazed at the vast numbers and variety of fencing stakes used by farmers. Notice too how the different piles are arranged not only by size, but by age, as the merchant won't sell his product until the wood has seasoned for a particular length of time.

Just before the end of the stacked timber, you will see an ornamental fishing lake on your left. Pass between wooden containers filled with gravel to join the right edge of **Barrow Wood** and keep forward.

The massive green barn-like building that you pass on the right is in fact a covered riding area. Similar buildings are often used for dressage training but in this case it is the venue for disabled riders who come for specialised lessons to Barrow Farm.

After **Barrow Farm** you will reach a road.

Cross over to follow a footpath indicated by a concrete finger-post. Ignore a fork left and go straight ahead.

Parsons Spring is a good example of coppiced woodland where the trees are cut right down to their bases and the new growth is harvested every ten years or so. This is an easier process than pollarding, where the lopping is at a height of 6 to 9 feet above the ground, but it does have the disadvantage that the new young shoots can be easily eaten – especially by deer. You will have seen the end product of this coppicing in the woodyard earlier.

After about ¼ mile you have open fields on your right. Continue along the edge until you reach a concrete track.

Turn left and follow this for ¼ mile to a road.

If you do this walk in the spring you will be rewarded with a fine show of daffodils along the track.

Cross the road into yet another

wood, **Birch Spring**.

This is a delightful mile-long woodland path. If you are alone or with a small, quiet group you are very likely to see deer here.

Eventually you will arrive at a spot where there is an open field on the left, a signpost, and tracks going right.

Continue forward with the field on the left and another coming into view on the right. Leave this wide track by passing through short white-painted posts. Continue on a drive, passing houses on the right to reach a cross-track.

Go right on a surfaced but pot-holed track, **Mapletree Lane**. You should have a wood on your left and a field, visible through trees, on your right.

Mapletree Lane is part of the St Peter's Way, a 44 mile walking route that starts at Chipping Ongar and finishes at the remote and ancient chapel of St Peter on the Wall at Bradwell.

After passing houses, the track curves to the left – on this bend there is a low barrier. Go right here, following a footpath sign with the **St Peter's Way** emblem on it. Join the path to recross **Millgreen Common** and return to your car.

18 Burnham-on-Crouch

The harbour at Burnham

The Walk 4 miles ⏱2½ hours
Map OS Explorer 176 Blackwater Estuary GR 953956

How to get there

From the A12 near Chelmsford you need to travel to either Maldon or South Woodham Ferrers. Whichever route you choose, you should join the B1010 which takes you right into Burnham-on-Crouch. On the outskirts turn right to pass the station. When the road swings to the left in the High Street look for the Clock Tower and, just before it, turn left up a narrow passage (Providence). The free car park is on the right. **Alternatively** you could park near the marina, which would mean starting the walk at point 8.

Drive and Stroll

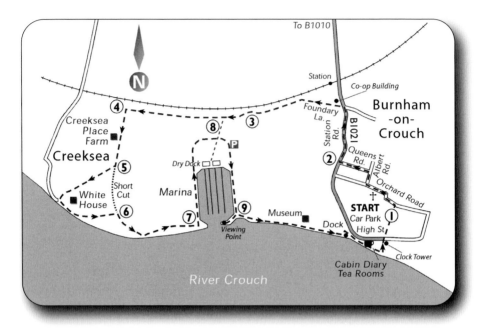

Introduction

If you are keen on boats, like rivers and enjoy expansive views – this is a walk for you. At first I take you up out of the town along quite ordinary roads with houses that are lovely to look at. The people of **Burnham** seem to take a real pride in their homes and a slightly milder climate, together with the large number of garden shops, combine to ensure that, even in the depths of winter, there are floral displays. After a mile or so you will be treated to tremendous views and then a descent to Creeksea where, according to legend, the Danish King Canute (Cnut) tried to command the sea to retreat and got his feet wet.

   The trip back to the port is all about boats – on the river, moored, and in dry dock. You finally arrive at the harbour with its ships' chandlers and terraces.

Refreshments

Besides boats, a main preoccupation in Burnham seems to be pubs. They are many and varied but all offer food of a reasonable standard. For those who prefer a café, I recommend the Cabin Diary Tea Rooms, a typically seaside affair (telephone: 01621 782404), and the Antiques Tea Room (telephone: 01621 786412), both of which you pass very near the end of the walk and where you can get simple home-cooked food and also Cornish cream teas.

THE WALK

NB: Although interesting and attractive, the circuit below **Creeksea** around the **White House** has several stiles in a short distance. This whole section (about ½ mile) can be missed out by simply carrying straight on (instead of turning right) at the end of point 4 and rejoining the main walk at point 6.

Leave the car park and turn right to walk up **Providence**. At the T-junction opposite **Nelson Court**, turn left along **Orchard Road** and follow this around to pass **St Cuthbert's Roman Catholic church** on your left. Turn right up **Albert Road**, then left along **Queen's Road** to its end.

Turn right to walk up **Station Road** until you reach a **Co-op building** with a clock tower. Turn left here to walk along **Foundry Lane**. After some time the road swings to the right; ignore and pass a footpath sign on the right that would take you across the railway. Soon after this, branch off left to walk along with a hedge on the right. Now you have views right across the **River Crouch** and its floodplains with **Southend-on-Sea** in the distance.

Keep this general direction to cross

a road and pass beside a strip of woodland on your right. Go through a barrier into a large arable field, and now the path continues with cypresses on the left. Diagonally left ahead you will see the buildings of **Creeksea Place Farm**.

At the end of the field, at a junction of paths, turn left to go down the side of the field and past the farm. Beyond the private entrance to a caravan park, turn right at a finger post. (Go straight on – see above – if you want to omit the **White House** section with its stiles, and continue from point 6.)

You follow a narrow path going alongside the caravan park to reach a drive. Go diagonally right to cross a stile on the left. Continue downhill with a wooden fence on your left, passing an attractive pond, to reach a stile into a drive. Cross this to a gate and maintain your direction down the left edge of a field. Another gate brings you to a narrow path with a hedge on the left and a fence on the right. You now pass houses, cross a drive and go over a stile on the left. You have at last reached the river's edge and are walking along an earthen sea wall. On your left are some fine houses. After passing a couple of jetties the wall curves inland to cut off a marshy area that is rich in birdlife. Cross a low barrier.

Drive and Stroll

Costly boats moored in the Burnham Marina

 ⑥

The sea wall swings to the right (just here you are joined by a path on the left – this is the path you would arrive by if you cut out the 'stile excursion').

At this point you can usually see quite large ships being loaded and unloaded, using cranes on the far bank. Ahead you can appreciate the extent of the area's love affair with boats. On a good day there must be over a thousand vessels in the channel and the marina, which we are approaching.

Continue for about ½ mile.

 ⑦

We are eventually forced to turn inland in order to negotiate the marina.

This marina, which is Britain's oldest, has a capacity of 500 boats and it is quite an education to be able to examine, at close quarters, what other people spend their hobby money on.

Continue up past the boats in the water, past the yachts in dry dock and beyond to join a narrow grassy path with a ditch on the left and a bank on the right. Where this path divides, go right up a steep bank and follow the path on the ground to reach a plateau. Cross towards wooded area to descend to the road that leads to the marina by a finger post.

Cross to a grassy path and turn right to walk with a large car park on your right.

Over a period of years, Maldon District Council is making money available for redefining and landscaping this area so it may be that this suggested route will change in some way. As long as it is realised that, essentially, all we are doing is walking around the three sides of the marina it is unlikely that anyone will go far wrong.

Continue walking down and keep forward on a surfaced path to join a promenade with benches on which you can relax and gaze at the boats in the marina.

At the end of this stretch you can turn right to walk out to a promontory on which there is a bench with rails that will stop you slipping into the water if you fall asleep.

The path now rejoins the **Crouch** and you walk towards **Burnham**. As you proceed, you can't fail to be struck by the improvement in the street furniture. Soon you will pass five sturdy houseboats – in spite of their size I wouldn't envy their inhabitants on a night with a heavy swell. The path, which is now brick-paved, passes various yacht and sailing clubs.

A considerable effort has been made to ensure that the new developments along this front successfully fit in with the surroundings.

Eventually the path turns inland to go around **Burnham Dock**. You turn right across the back of the dock to pass **Priors Boatyard** on the right and emerge alongside the **Cabin Diary Tea Rooms**. Keep on along the front, past the **Tourist Information Centre**, along a delightful terrace, and turn left just before the Anchor Hotel. You will emerge on the **High Street**; go slightly right to the narrow street of **Providence** opposite. The car park is up here on the right, just past the **Queen's Head**.

19 | Leigh-on-Sea

Hadleigh Castle

The Walk 4¼ miles ⊕ Allow 2½ hours
Map OS Explorer 175 Southend-on-Sea & Basildon GR 829856

How to get there

Make for Leigh-on-Sea Station by turning south off the A13. Drive past the station, over the railway, past the station car park on the right and look for a small (free) parking area about 300 yards further on, on the left. **Alternatively** if this is full or you want added security, the station car park has a cheap rate after 10 am and on Saturdays and Sundays. If you choose to park here, start the walk by going slightly left out of the car park, crossing the road, climbing steps and turning right to walk along the sea wall.

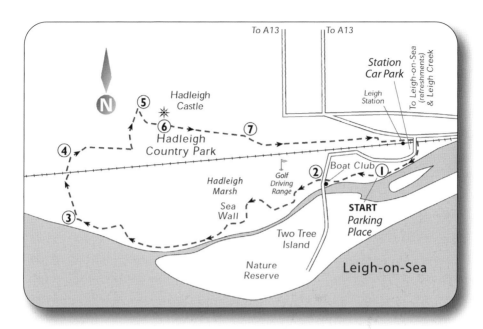

Introduction

This walk, along part of the Essex coastline, starts in a fairly standard way. It has the stranded boats, the mud flats and a huge range of birds. Inland you get good sightings of kestrels, herons and avocets. On the mud flats the waders are sometimes numbered in their thousands. However, it is the second half, starting with an exploration of Hadleigh Castle, that makes this outing really memorable. The stroll back to **Leigh-on-Sea** will delight on a clear day and work up an appetite for the seafood to follow.

Refreshments

If you don't mind walking another ¼ mile (and back again) you could leave the car where it is. You go up past the station and turn right and right again to follow a road over the railway line. This becomes a narrow street between attractive cottages, galleries, pubs, restaurants and cafés. It is a dead end but there is limited parking. You can get standard café fare at either the Strand Tea Rooms or Sara's Tea Garden but I recommend you mark the occasion with seafood. There are several stalls but the best way to enjoy your cockles, whelks, smoked sprats etc is opposite the Crooked Billet pub. Here tables and benches are set out alongside the Osborne Brothers' Quality Shellfish Stall – so you can buy your pint, cross the road, pick up a selection of seafood delights and munch and drink overlooking Leigh Creek.

Drive and Stroll

THE WALK

Leave the car parking area at the back, walk up steps to the sea wall and turn right.

You now have most of the conditions that will dominate the walk for the next couple of miles. To the left, across mud flats, you can see Canvey Island. Further on are the fractionating towers of Shell Haven and ahead are the ruins of Hadleigh Castle, which will be the focus for the outward journey.

Continue for about ½ mile.

Eventually you will reach a surfaced cross-track with a boat club on the left (you could go left here onto **Two Tree Island** – a signed 1 mile path will take you around the nature reserve there). Go straight across the road, past metal gates, and continue forward along a surfaced path with a golf driving range on your right.

As is so often the case, the channel left by excavations for the sea wall provides an interesting contrast with the mud flats on the left. The waterfowl on the right are numerous but in no way match the numbers of waders on the left. If you want to vary the walk you can descend to the channel edge where you will find a path – it is not sensible to do this on the left as the marsh and mud can be dangerous.

After about 2 miles of following the route of the sea wall you will come to a gate. A notice announces that you are entering **Hadleigh Castle Country Park**.

About 50 yards after the gate, turn right and walk down the bank to a stile and continue across a field. Go over the busy railway line with care at the crossing and bear slightly right to the corner of the field on the other side.

Go through two gates and up a bank, then walk along the lower edge of the field with trees and a hedge on your right. At a waymarker keep forward over a stile on a fenced path to emerge on the left edge of a field, walking parallel with the railway. Continue across an open field to cross another stile and walk left uphill, with the hedge on your left, to join a track.

At the top of the hill, cross a stile and go right through a metal gate. Climb up a path to the right of a mound ahead of you to reach the castle.

Hadleigh Castle is an impressive stone keep and bailey fortress, with the remains of a barbican and two

Leigh from the outward track along the marsh

flanking towers on the curtain wall. Once considered a strategically important fortress for protecting the approach to London via the Thames Estuary, the castle was extensively repaired and rebuilt under Edward III in the 1360s. A series of landslips have seriously undermined the wall and towers. John Constable painted a famous picture of it in 1829 but you will have to visit America to see it.

You will undoubtedly want to spend time wandering around the ruins, but when you decide to leave do so between the towers, walking downhill to a gate at the bottom.

 ⑥

Now go ahead along the ridge.

This is the most spectacular part of the walk – at this height you can see beyond Canvey Island to the Thames Estuary. Here there will

generally be a large number of ships waiting to pass up the Thames or on their way out. Ahead, Leigh-on-Sea is laid out before you and in the distance you should be able to see the mile-long Southend Pier stretching out into the sea.

All too soon, the ridge descends to a stile.

 ⑦

Here you leave the country park and continue round the left edge of the next field. At a fork, continue forward with scrub to the left. Towards the end of this field fork slightly right to a road. Go right off this over a grassy area to reach the station. Pass the station and turn right. Just before the entrance to its car park cross the road and turn right on the sea wall path. After a short distance you will return to the parking area.

20 Hainault Forest

Geese grazing on the plain near the lake

The Walk 5½ miles or 3½ miles if you opt for just the southern section of this figure of eight route (see map) 🕒 3 hours
Map OS Explorer 174 Epping Forest & Lee Valley GR 471936

How to get there

Hainault Forest is to the east of Chigwell Row, which is near Chigwell and is best reached by coming off the M11 at junction 5 (but note that you cannot rejoin it here). The car park is a short distance on a minor road which goes north-east from the junction of the B173 and the A1112 at Chigwell Row. The entrance is directly opposite Chigwell Row Infants' School. **Alternatively** you could use the car park opposite the Miller & Carter pub – in this case you would start the walk at point 6.

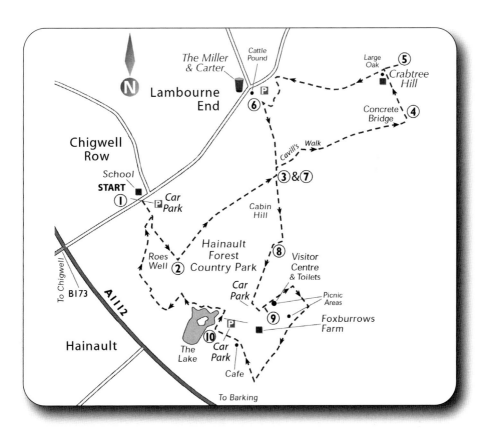

Introduction

The Normans really enjoyed their hunting and **Hainault Forest** is one of three remnants of their sporting arena linked by the Three Forests Way. Although this is the smallest forest of the group this walk still spends most of its time winding its way through the attractive hornbeam-dominated woodland, far away from the din of traffic but occasionally interrupted by propeller-driven aircraft from the nearby aerodrome. As bonuses the walk provides a visit to a large lake packed with waterfowl and a highpoint, especially if you bring children, of a visit to **Foxburrows Farm** which specialises in rare breeds.

Refreshments

There is a café at the end of point 9 and this sells a full range of snacks and fast foods. The Miller & Carter pub is opposite a car park at point 6. Here you can purchase a variety of food, from snacks to full meals (telephone: 02085 007712).

Drive and Stroll

THE WALK

NB: A look at the map will show you that this is a figure of eight route. You could shorten the walk to one of 3½ miles by turning right at the end of point 2 and continuing with the directions from point 7.

Leave the car park, going past an information board, with houses on the right and a meadow on the left. On the edge of woodland go right and immediately fork left – taking the centre of the three paths available. Keep forward on a wide track, ignoring side paths to eventually reach a stony cross-path.

Turn left and start walking uphill (you may find it more exciting to walk up inside the woodland on the left – if you do so, keep in touch with this main path from time to time).

Towards the top of the hill you can see, on the left, the remains of some Victorian metal fencing. In some cases you may notice that trees have actually incorporated the fence into their trunks.

The path flattens out and eventually delivers you to a clearing. This is **Cabin Hill.**

(If you are doing the short walk, go right to the left of a map-board downhill on a grassy track and continue with stage 7.) For the full route, at the junction of five paths you take the first on the left to the left of an interpretation board. Go forward for about 40 yards to turn right on a path with a waymarker in memory of James Cavill.

As you can see from the inscription, James Cavill, a wheelwright, was born in 1802 and lived in Abridge Cottage in nearby Chigwell Row for 86 years. The path's dedication was researched and financed by descendants who now live in Western Australia.

At the next junction fork right over a barrier and continue forward, ignoring all side paths.

The care of Hainault Forest has recently passed into the hands of the Woodland Trust. The wood hasn't been harvested for generations and, as a result, some trees have assumed grotesque shapes. If you enjoy a fright, you may like to consider doing this part of the walk at night, during the wintertime, with a full moon.

After some time the path descends and you can glimpse open countryside on the right. As you approach a barrier with open countryside beyond, turn left through a kissing gate alongside a seven-bar gate. You should now be walking just within the right-hand edge of the wood. Continue downhill to a point where there are bridges ahead and to the right – ignore both, going immediately left. On this narrow path you have a watercourse to the right which you soon cross via a stone bridge.

You should now be walking inside the right-hand edge of woodland with the ditch on your left. Keep climbing until you pass through a gate and are confronted by a large oak. Turn right here to lean on a five-bar gate and look at the view.

On the left you may have noticed a metal London County Council boundary post – given that we are several miles outside the boundary of the old LCC you may think that this has been planted here by someone with a warped sense of humour. A campaign to purchase the Forest and preserve it was £10,000 short in 1903 when the LCC came to the rescue and agreed to manage it for the people forever. The Greater London Council took overall responsibility from its formation in 1964 until its demise, when the London Borough of Redbridge took control for Havering and Essex.

Ahead you can see **Stapleford Abbots** and over to the right is **Havering church** with a white water tower to the left.

Turn away from the viewpoint and return to the oak. Fork right to walk downhill, past houses and keep with this track as it climbs again. After nearly ½ mile you come to a gate beyond which is a road; immediately turn left along a surfaced ride. Stay with this as it describes an irregular semicircle and brings you to a car park. Opposite the car park on the other side of the road is the **Miller & Carter** public house. Within the car park on the left is a Victorian cattle pound where stray beasts were kept.

With your back to the gate of the car park, go straight ahead on a beautiful, broad woodland path.

This section is good at any time of the year but, for me, the best time is the winter when, bereft of leaves, the trees reveal their skeletal shapes.

At the end of this path you reach the complicated cross paths at the clearing which you will recognise from your outward journey

Keep forward, through a fence, to descend over grass to a hollow on the right. Go right, keeping to the higher path. Cross a clearing to swing left in woodland to emerge on an open plain by a beacon.

Go straight towards a car park in the distance. When you reach the car park turn left and walk up to a road. Here turn left, then right to visit **Foxburrows Farm**.

This is always a great hit with children because they can see 'ordinary' animals up close. Usually you will be able to look at rabbits, goats, pheasants, turkeys, pigs, donkeys, lots of strange sheep and Highland cattle. The farm opens daily at 9 am and closes at 5 pm from April to September; in the winter months it closes at 3 pm. There is a petting area open between 1.30 pm and 3 pm on Saturday and Sunday afternoons. Outside opening times, you can see most of the animals quite easily.

Rejoin the road with the farm, visitor centre and toilets to the right. Go past a dog-free picnic area and a short terrace of houses. Just before a black barn-like building, turn right to walk uphill with a mesh fence on the right. The path swings away from the golf course on the left and you soon gain views of the farm and parkland over to the right. At the top of the hill you pass another picnic area and possibly some Highland cattle on your right. Keep forward, passing a path signed to the visitor centre and, at first, hugging a wicket fence on your left and later joining a twin wire fence on the right. When the woodland finishes, turn right through a gap in the wire and walk out over parkland, aiming for the right of a distant lake. As you get closer, to the right of a car park, you will see two low buildings – go between these (a café and toilets) to go through a barrier on a surfaced path to the lake.

Where the path swings left, take a narrower path to the right, then fork left over a bridge and go left at a T-junction to join the wooden-fenced edge of the lake. Follow the path as it swings away into woodland. Now go slightly right, following a waymarker for the **London Loop** and, in about 40 yards, turn left over a wide bridge. Go forward on this track as it swings left and right and over a crosstrack. Pass an elaborate rope exercise area on the left to reach an array of paths. Take the first narrow path on the right between young trees. Cross a gap in a fence to reach a T-junction and turn right to soon reach a major junction with a finger-post. Go left on 'Retreat Path'. After about 300 yards you come to a bench and a ride on the right. Follow this to pass round **Roes Well**, going forward and turning left, back up the path to the car park.